GHOST STORIES of TENNESSEE

A.S. Mott

LONE PINE

Lone Pine Publishing International

The Publisher: Lone Pine Publishing International
Distributed by Lone Pine Publishing
1808 B Street NW, Suite 140
Auburn, WA 98001
USA

Websites: www.lonepinepublishing.com
www.ghostbooks.net

National Library of Canada Cataloguing in Publication Data

Mott, A. S. (Allan S.), 1975-
   Ghost stories of Tennessee / A.S. Mott.

   ISBN-13: 978-1-894877-72-5
   ISBN-10: 1-894877-72-1

   1. Ghosts--Tennessee. 2. Tales--Tennessee. I. Title.

GR110.T4M68 2005   398.2'09768'05   C2005-904484-5

Photo Credits: Every effort has been made to accurately credit photographers. Any errors or omissions should be directed to the publisher for changes in future editions. The photographs and illustrations in this book are reproduced with the kind permission of the following sources: Istock (p. 9; p. 77: Lise Gagne; p. 103: Bradley Mason; p. 110: Norman Eder; p. 145, 167: Dan Brandenburg; p. 149: P. Sigin-Lavdanski; p. 152: Bryce Kroll; p. 186: Brent Nelson; p. 193: Kevin Britland); Library of Congress (p. 4-5: HAER, TENN,033-CHAT.V,1-15; p. 11: USZ62-7041; p. 15: D4-39517; p. 31: USZ62-98163; p. 62: HABS, TENN,19-NASH,20-2; p. 65: HABS, TENN,19-NASH,20-23; p. 86, 88: HAER, TENN,033-CHAT.V,1-6); North Wind Picture Archives (p. 27).

The stories, folklore and legends in this book are based on the author's collection of sources including individuals whose experiences have led them to believe they have encountered phenomena of some kind or another. They are meant to entertain, and neither the publisher nor the author claims these stories represent fact.

PC: P5

To My Mom

*Who used to scream with her friends
whenever she saw Elvis on-screen*

CONTENTS

Acknowledgments

Thanks to my editors Carol Woo and Rachelle Delaney for being kind when others would have been cruel. Thanks to Trina Koscielnuk for compiling this text into a recognizable book-like form and to Gerry Dotto for giving it a cover. And a very overdue thanks to Frank, who cooks our lunches; to Donna, our receptionist; to Mary and her crackerjack office staff; to Dana and the warehouse crew; to Dave and all the fine folks in sales; to Ken and his Four Marketeers; to my fellow authors and to everyone in production and editorial who has yet to be thanked in one of my books. Without any of you this book would not exist.

Introduction

What makes for a good ghost story? Having written my seventh paranormal book, I have concluded that a good ghost story requires at least two of the following elements:

1. A ghost or some other sort of supernatural creature
2. An intriguing back story explaining the origin of said ghost/supernatural creature
3. A once-skeptical living person whose experience with the ghost/supernatural creature has a profound effect on their life
4. The Civil War
5. A celebrity
6. A landmark
7. Sex

Now number one is a given. You can't have a ghost story without a ghost (believe me I've tried and I've been called on it every single time). Number two is less essential but whenever I have a choice between writing about the ghost of some boring guy who died in some boring way over, let's say, the ghost of a monk who died in a train crash and whose body was then stolen by a small-town doctor to replace his missing medical skeleton, I'll go with the monk every single time. Number three is pretty important as well because without it you're often left with that old Zen koan "If a ghost haunts a house and there is no one there to see or hear it, does it make a story?" Number four might seem a bit more odd, but trust me it's true.

Number five is pretty self-explanatory. Any story about a celebrity ghost is bound to be helped by requirement number two, and even if it isn't, the recognition factor often works wonders. The same is true for number six where a famous person is replaced by a famous piece of property. And as for number seven... well... a little sex appeal always makes these stories a little more interesting.

In writing these stories I made certain dramatic liberties here and there, but often no such liberties were required as there is often nothing more fascinating than the truth. Some stories are based on Tennessee folklore, other stories transformed into something that is neither as reality or fiction and is often referred to as legend, while others tell of some of the most well-documented hauntings in the history of the United States.

Is there any profound theme that you can glean from these stories? I don't think so, but then that was never my intention. I would hope instead that this book causes you to at some point laugh or cry or feel a chill run down your spine. If it does, then I would consider this book a success and my theories about telling good ghost stories to be perfectly sound.

1
Historical Hauntings

A Tour Down Through the River of Blood

The Cherokee called this place Chickamauga, and they were right to do so, for in their language it means "river of blood" and never has a place been more worthy of so horrible a name. The year was 1863 and America was a land at war. On this soiled spot, not far from the town of Chattanooga, 35,000 men died in a battle that raged for three days in September; the anger and hatred that spewed out over this site forever infected this land with an aura of pain and terror. It should come as no surprise that this is a place where spirits, phantoms and ghosts come to mourn, remember and—most importantly—avenge.

The first thing you will notice is the fog. To stand in it is like being in a bonfire without the flame; the smell of ash is overpowering in the thick, white mist. Some say the fog is what remains of the smoke that billowed out of the cannon and muskets as the battle carved, slashed and mutilated its way across these lush, green fields, and it lingers to remind us of the folly of men. Still others claim that the fog is not a fog at all, but a collection of lost souls so great in number that it is impossible not to see it with the naked eye. Just one of these souls would be invisible to our senses, but gathered together in such a concentrated mass, they form a cloud of mist that even the greatest skeptic cannot ignore. Whichever theory is true, those who are brave enough to walk through the haze

On this soiled spot, 35,000 men died in the Battle of Chicakamauga.

claim to hear the sound of mournful cries and pitiful wails of sorrow.

Others insist they have seen the ghosts of individual soldiers in the fog, whose misty cover serves as a shelter from the burning rays of the sun—the same sun that set alight the land where they once allowed themselves to be led to such ignoble slaughter. And there are some people who say that it is merely fog and nothing else, and claim that those who say otherwise are suckers and fools. But they seldom say this for too long, because very often they will see or hear something that will quickly change their minds.

Perhaps the distant sounds of cannon blasting or the hollow pop of gunshots convinces them. Or maybe they will hear the shouts of men who died over 140 years ago begging to see their mothers for one last time or for the pain—the searing, bloody pain—to stop, please stop. If they are still not convinced, they should be advised to come once again in the cool, autumn month of September.

It is during September—and September alone—that one can expect to see the spirit known only as The Lady in White. She is named for the bridal gown she wears as she walks the park's green fields in search of the man who she was supposed to marry. No one knows her name or the name of the man she seeks. She speaks to no one and will not notice you if you are nearby. She is too busy searching—always searching. Every September since 1863 she has gone on this quest, and each September ends with her mission unfulfilled.

She is a beauty with blond hair and the pale features to match her simple but elegant wedding dress. She is a symbol of hope and despair. Someday she will find her love. Someday they will be reunited. Someday she will never have to walk along the "river of blood" ever again, and when that day comes, her despair, which can be felt by all who are near it each September, will turn to joy and maybe, for one short, shining moment, the park—this monument to death—could be a happy place once again.

The Lady in White is not the only ghost to walk this land; there is another who knows nothing about hope and exists only to cause despair. Some call it spirit, others call it demon; all call it Old Green Eyes and no one wants to know any more about the creature than that. For to know more, you would have to see it, and to see it can likely mean your doom.

How this foul creature came to haunt the park is still not known. Some claim it is the ghost of a Union soldier who was killed in the battle by his own brother, a Confederate, while others insist it is far older than the famous battle for which the land got its gruesome name. They believe that Old Green Eyes is not a ghost, but a creature of palpable flesh and blood. Its arms, legs and body are that of a man, but from there all similarities to humanity are said to end. Its hair is dyed red with the blood of all those who have faced the creature and not lived to tell the tale. Its eyes are a queasy orange-tinted green, like a decaying swamp that has been set on fire. Its teeth are that of a wild animal's, sharp and jagged, covered in blood and tiny rotting pieces of flesh.

No two descriptions of its face are alike. Those who have seen the creature and survived were far too frightened by what they saw to take a note of its inhuman features. Once a camera almost captured a glimpse of the creature's monstrous visage, but before the film could be developed, the camera was dropped and all of the photographs it contained were lost.

Two cars were said to have crashed in an attempt to avoid two horrible green eyes that appeared suddenly in the middle of the road. But at least the men behind the wheels of those cars were not injured in their encounter with the monster with the blood red hair. The same cannot be said for a poor teenage boy who encountered the creature in the summer of 1970.

The boy, who we will call Ed, had spent most of the day with his friends, drinking beer and urging one another on to commit a series of increasingly stupid and highly dangerous dares. A friend of his suggested that they go to Chickamauga to look for ghosts. His friend went on to tell them all about the legend of Old Green Eyes, which all of them dismissed as a hilariously foolish fairy tale. Ed, especially, found the story amusing and couldn't stop laughing when he heard it, so his friend dared him to go to Chickamauga and prove that Old Green Eyes did not exist. Ed agreed and they all headed over to the park so he could make his friend look like a fool.

When they got there, they spent a drunken hour wandering around the park, making fun of their superstitious friend by pretending to be scared. But they stopped playing this game when they came across an old tower that none of them knew existed.

Built out of stone and standing 85 feet high, the tower had been built in 1903 to honor the memory of General John Wilder, a Union soldier who, when he discovered that his men lacked the supplies they needed to go into battle, spent $25,000 of his own money to make sure they were properly equipped. But the drunken teenagers saw the tower more as a novelty to be explored rather than a monument.

The door to the tower was locked, but Ed and his friends were far too intoxicated to let that stop them from getting inside. They looked up and saw what looked like a series of little windows along the sides of the tower. They were actually gun turrets, built to symbolize the rifles that had been purchased thanks to the general's donation, and they appeared to be the best bet to get inside. When the tower's face proved impossible to climb, Ed noticed that a lightning rod was attached to one side of the structure. He

Wilder Tower Monument

started shimmying up the rod and only had to go up 14 feet before he found an open turret. He climbed into and shouted down to his friends to come up and join him.

But before they could follow him, a terrifying sound was heard coming from inside the tower. It was a horrible nightmarish sound that was immediately followed by the equally horrible sound of Ed screaming. His friends watched aghast as he threw himself out of one of the turrets. In his panic he had become confused and, instead of jumping out of the turret from which he entered, he leaped out of one that was 25 feet off the ground. He expected to grab the lightning rod, but it wasn't where he thought it was, so he fell all the way down on the concrete ground below.

He lived, but he never walked again. When people asked him what scared him enough to take that leap, he never answered them. He refused to say that it was Old Green Eyes, but his friends could see the truth in his eyes. None of them ever went to Chickamauga again.

Six years later the tower was once again the site of a strange incident when a ceremony was held to commemorate the country's bicentennial in 1977. When the tower had been built 74 years before, the veterans who financed its construction placed important mementos of their lives and of the war in which they fought into a time capsule. They hoped that a future generation would open it and be given a greater understanding of their past. It had been decided that the bicentennial ceremony was the perfect time to retrieve and open the capsule, so, with much fanfare, the cornerstone in which that capsule had been placed was removed. Jubilation quickly grew into shock and outrage when all that was revealed was an empty hole. The capsule was gone along with everything that it contained. An investigation followed, and to everyone's frustration, no evidence of theft or previous tampering could be found. It didn't take long for people to attribute the crime to Old Green Eyes, although some suspected that other spirits could also be responsible, most likely a dead Confederate soldier chagrined to have spend eternity so close to a monument to a Union general.

If a dead rebel soldier were responsible for this crime, it would be hard to blame him. The name given to this land by the Cherokee was not symbolic, but rather an honest description of what it looked like during those three horrible days in September 1863. This land was literally covered with a river of blood as 35,000 men were killed. That a massacre of this size to leave an impact on this land should come as no surprise. What should seem shocking instead is that the spirits allow the park any peace at all.

A Tennessee Plantation

Kingsport, Tennessee's Rotherwood Mansion is one of those places that instantly evokes memories of a time and place that really only exist in our nostalgic collective unconsciousness. With its white Roman pillars and classic southern Gothic design, it's easy to imagine it being a place where Scarlett O'Hara could turn window drapes into a new gown and where Rhett Butler could tell her that he doesn't give a damn about what fate was in store for her. But history has a way of doing everything it can to dispel our romantic notions of simpler, less complicated times, and the lesson that we can learn from the ghosts that haunt this large plantation estate is that life for some—no matter what the time and place—has always been a difficult row to hoe.

The mansion was built in 1818 by a reverend named Frederick A. Ross. He was a pious man who helped built the town that would eventually become Kingsport, which at the time was named Rossville in his honor. He had much to be proud of, and the one jewel that he could claim as his greatest source of pride was his daughter Roweena.

Roweena was an extraordinary young woman. Both kind and beautiful, she was also intelligent, having spent years in the best schools the North had to offer. Women found her charming and never felt threatened by her gifts, while men were instantly attracted to her unique presence, which was unlike any other that could be found in the county's burgeoning social sphere. Her potential suitors were numerous, but she never gave into the temptation to flirt or tease. Instead, she made it clear that her heart belonged to one man, a medical student and amateur sailor named Nathanial.

Everyone who had ever seen them together knew that they were a couple destined for greatness. He had proposed to her, but she had insisted that they wait until he graduated from school before they got married. She, more than anyone, knew how important it was for a person to complete his or her education and she did not want anything to derail her fiancé from becoming a doctor.

But it was not to be. Nathanial's love of sailing came at a tragic cost. As Roweena watched his boat sail one afternoon in the Holston River, which flowed not far from Rotherwood, she was horrified to see it suddenly tip over and capsize. Nathanial fell into the water and his body was never found. Roweena was haunted by this tragedy. To her, it had appeared as though the river itself had decided to kill her love, as if it was meting out the punishment for an uncollected debt he had never told her about. In an instant the grace and charisma that had made her so popular with everyone she had known vanished in a tidal wave of grief. She hid herself inside Rotherwood and refused to come out for two full years.

When she did finally emerge from the house, she was a pale shadow of what she once was. She was still beautiful, but her charm had faded and she seemed barely capable of engaging in the simplest of conversations, much less trade the witty banter for which she had once been renown. That was why so many were surprised to hear that not long after her return to society, she was once

again engaged. This time her fiancé was a rich business-
man from Knoxville. His name was Truman, and though
Roweena could never love him as she did Nathanial, his
patience and kindness were such that he seemed as good
for her as she could ever expect to find.

But then, just a week after their wedding, Truman
became ill. He had contracted yellow fever and he died
just a few days later. Knowing how she had reacted the
first time tragedy had struck her life, few people believed
Roweena would ever recover from this second romantic
catastrophe. And for a full decade it appeared as though
they were right. Ten years passed without a day in which
she did not grieve, but then one morning she awoke and
realized that—as if someone had stolen it during the
night—her grief was gone. Those who had known her
before the death of Nathanial were astounded to see the
woman they had once adored return, as if she had simply
gone on a long, 12-year holiday. Within a month she had
found another fiancé—a doctor named Paul—and nine
months after their wedding she gave birth to their daughter, Lorraine.

For several years they lived at Rotherwood, as happy as
any family could be, but when Lorraine turned six,
Roweena began to hear another person's voice in her
head. It was Nathanial. He was calling to her, begging her
to join him in his watery grave. For weeks she pretended
not to hear him and gave no indication to her family that
anything was wrong, but soon Nathanial's voice became
too persuasive. Her true love was urging her to remove
herself from this mortal coil and join him in paradise

forever. Roweena headed toward the Holston River to be with him.

The first time she tried, she was stopped before she drowned. Paul and her father were heartbroken to learn that—despite what the past six years of her life had indicated—she had never gotten over Nathanial's death and her sublimated grief had caused her to lose her mind.

She was kept in her room, but one night the nurse who was hired to watch over her became distracted and she was able to slip away. She left the mansion and ran to the river. By the time the nurse discovered that she was gone, Roweena was in the water, on her way to Nathanial. Her body was found on the river's edge. On her cold, lifeless face was a satisfied smile.

But in the days that followed her death, it became clear that she and Nathanial were not successfully reunited. People reported having encounters with both of their spirits. At least one witness saw Roweena walking along the banks of the river in a white wedding dress while Nathanial's voice was heard calling out from the river, which suggested to some that Roweena had never lost her mind at all.

Reports of their presence at Rotherwood continue to this day, but theirs are not the only otherworldly presences to be found around the mansion's grounds. By 1847, Reverend Ross' fortunes had fallen and he was forced to sell the home he had built almost 30 years earlier. The man who bought it from him was as different from the Reverend as night is to day. His name was Joshua Phipps and he was as cruel and evil a man as the South had ever known.

Phipps was able to satisfy his sadistic desires by torturing the men and women he was legally able to call his property. An example of his sickness could be found inside Rotherwood, which now housed a whipping post in one of its rooms, where the monster could whip his slaves without having to go outside to do it.

Phipps' behavior was not tolerated in the community, but there was nothing anyone could legally do to stop him. He was eventually shunned by nearly all of Kingsport's populace, so when he became ill, in 1861, no one felt any sadness. As he lay dying, he ordered that one of his slaves stay with him and fan him with a leaf to help soothe his constant fever. Hours later, Phipps was found dead, but it appeared that he had not been taken by his illness, but he instead had been suffocated while he slept. The slave who had been fanning him was charged with his murder, but the poor young man insisted that he was innocent. But if he did not do it, then who did? The man was hesitant to say, but when it became clear he would be hanged if he did not tell his strange tale, he finally relented and told the authorities what had happened.

"I was standing there, fanning Mr. Phipps, when a swarm of flies flew through his window and surrounded his head. He tried to swat them all away, but there were hundreds of them! They went in his mouth and his nose and he couldn't breathe! Then, as soon as he was dead, they flew away."

At first everyone thought the story was merely just a desperate alibi devised by a man who knew he was sure to hang for his crime, but then—just to be safe—Phipps body was examined, and to the police's amazement, dead flies could be found in both his nose and his mouth. But sadly, in a turn that would have brought joy to Phipps' cold, sadistic heart, this evidence that gave credence to the man's story was ignored and he was hanged after a trial that barely lasted a full half hour.

Because of his infamy around the county, Phipps' funeral was a highly attended affair. Some people came out of curiosity, while many more came to make sure that the evil bastard was really dead. Everyone was there to watch when the horse-drawn hearse pulling his casket suddenly stopped on the way to the grave site, as if its cargo had suddenly become too heavy to pull.

The sky above began to grow dark and thunder roared as lightning flashed in the distance. More horses were added to the front of the carriage, but even then it was a struggle to get the hearse to Phipps' grave. The rain began to fall just as the carriage reached the site, and though the bad weather was convincing many of the casual onlookers to return home, hundreds of people remained to see what happened next. As two of the undertakers started pushing the casket out of the hearse, it began to shake in their hands. To their astonishment, it burst open and out leapt a large black dog. The evil-looking animal growled menacingly at all those present before running toward the Rotherwood Plantation.

After Phipps' death, the house fell into the hands of his mistress, Hetty, a former slave who showed no sympathy at all to those who were unfortunate enough to be in her former situation. If anything, she proved to be a more sadistic taskmaster than her dead lover had been. But this time, the men and women who were forced to work the plantation decided not to wait for a swarm of mysterious flies to rid them of their abuser, and so they rose up against her and murdered her in her sleep. They buried her in an unmarked grave on the plantation's grounds, not long before the Civil War ended and slavery was finally abolished.

Since then, the ghosts of Joshua Phipps, his mistress and the demonic black dog—known around the area as the Hound of Hell—have all been spotted around the Rotherwood Plantation, making for a total of five phantoms said to be attached to this historically beautiful site. It isn't surprising then that many of Kingsport's residents choose to avoid the area at night. With so many spirits haunting the land, the odds of running into a sinister presence is simply too great for any sane person to risk.

One has to wonder about a place where so much tragedy has occurred. Was the plantation cursed right from the start? Or did years of spiritual darkness finally take their toll on the land? Or is it all a horrible coincidence? Whatever the answer, the truth remains clear: the romantic past we have seen so often celebrated in books and on film really only exists in our minds. The reality is that life has never been as simple and easy as we would like to remember.

Suck Creek

Yes, there really is a place called Suck Creek. It's a small rural community nestled on the edge of the Prentice Cooper Wildlife Management Area in Tennessee's Marion County. It is named for the body of water that flows through the area, one whose currents cause potentially dangerous whirlpools when they meet the waters of the Tennessee River. Many boats have sunk in these dangerous waters, but none of these wrecks have had as large a paranormal impact on the community as one shocking incident that occurred in those savage days when a man could still be considered another man's property.

The ghost is said to haunt Cumberland Trail where this tragic spirit was crushed and beaten for the crime of wanting to be free. Though the man's name has been lost to time, it was known that he was a slave owned by one of the cruelest and most violent men in the entire county. This man, by the standards of our present morality, would be considered a psychopathic monster, a serial killer with dozens of victims to his name. But because all of his victims were slaves, he was never once tried for murder or even considered a despicable man by those who knew him. His cruelty was considered a flaw, but he was not shunned or feared by his community.

One of his favorite acts of cruelty was to assign a slave an impossible task, such as giving him a single afternoon to pick a whole field of cotton without any help. He would tell the slave about the horrible whipping they would receive if the task was not completed in the time he allotted, and then he would sit and watch with a sinister delight as the sun started to set. His poor victim, who had struggled mightily all alone in the field, would begin to visibly panic over the thought of the beating they were about to endure. Most men could not afford to be so cruel, as slaves cost money, but he was a very wealthy man and could easily replenish his stock when his torture took an inevitably fatal toll.

You would think that a master so cruel would have to deal with attempted escapes by his slaves each and every day, but such attempts actually occurred only on the very rarest of occasions. The reason for this was simple; those who did try to escape and were unsuccessful met fates that could only be considered worse than death. One man had both of his thumbs cut off before being sent out back to the fields, where he collapsed dead from exhaustion, dehydration and hunger. And his was one of the less severe punishments meted out to someone who wanted only their freedom.

But for the spirit that haunts Cumberland Trail, there was no punishment too severe to keep him from attempting to get away from this insanity. He made his run for freedom during the middle of a scorching hot summer night. He was desperate to escape even though he had no idea where he could go or what he would find in the woods that surrounded the creek. He soon found himself running down the trail, hoping that it would lead him somewhere where he could hide. He didn't like how the trail was so open, but the woods were too thick for any man to move through them with any speed.

By the time the sun started to rise, the man was exhausted and could not run another step. He walked off

Slaves picking cotton

the trail and found a spot where he hoped he would be able to hide until he felt strong enough to get up and continue. Just as he was lying down, his absence was discovered on the farm. The master and his hired hands—whose cruelty nearly matched his own—reacted by throwing leashes on their bloodhounds and taking the animals to the spot where the man usually slept. The dogs captured his scent right away and started pulling the men toward the woods and down the trail. Word spread around the community that a slave had escaped and other men from nearby farms joined the master and his hands in their search.

In his hiding spot in the woods, the hunted man slept for far longer than was wise to do. He was just so tired that his body simply would not let him rise. By the time he heard the sound of dogs and men in the distance, he knew it was too late. He rose and started to run, but he was still so tired that he only made it for an hour before he collapsed onto the trail. He was still lying there when the mob found him. Together they beat and thrashed him before a rope was thrown over a nearby tree. Unconscious after their assault, the man did not feel it the noose on his neck, and when the rope was pulled up, his feet dangled helplessly in the air.

The man was left to hang as the mob dispersed and its bloodthirsty associates returned to their farms. And at this point the story almost has a happy ending because—as if by a miracle—the man awoke while he dangled from the tree. Somehow the noose was tied in a way that it did not cut off his oxygen and he was able to loosen it from his neck and fall back down to the ground. His body was horribly beaten and some of his bones were broken, but he still had the will to run and—since they thought he was dead—there was a chance that this time he might make it.

But the story does not have a happy ending. When the cruel master returned to his farm he realized that this escaped slave's fate was not a sufficient example to anyone else who might also think of running for their freedom. He and his hands turned back to retrieve the slave's body so he could mutilate it and display it in front of all those who knew and worked with the man. When they returned to the spot where the man had been hanged, they were shocked to find only a noose swinging in the wind, but it didn't take them long to find its former occupant crawling slowly down the trail.

This time they took no chances and made sure to beat the man until he was dead. They took his body back to the farm and did unspeakable things to it before displaying it right in front of the small shack the other slaves called home.

And while it would be most just to tell you that this cruel master was soon punished for his vile crimes, this is simply and sadly a case where justice was never served. The man lived to a ripe old age before dying peacefully in his sleep. The Emancipation Proclamation ensured that his reign of terror did eventually end, but he never faced any punishment for the crimes he committed during a time where it was considered proper for men to own other men.

Sadly, this horrible injustice keeps the spirit of the man who died attempting to win his freedom from leaving the trail where he was cruelly and callously murdered. He yearns to find the men who killed him and show them the true meaning of the word fear, but they are all long dead and their spirits have passed on from this world.

Those who have walked the woods have heard his groans echo around them. The pain that he endures is evident in every agonizing gasp, but it is not the pain of his wounds that causes him to cry out this way. It is the pain, instead, of being compelled to complete his impossible task. Like the poor slave alone in the cotton field who knew that no matter how hard he worked, he would be beaten once the sun comes down, this broken man carries on not because he wants to, but because he has to. He continues to search for justice, even when it appears to be futile.

Some have not just heard him; they have seen him, limping slowly as a mist along the trail. All those who have witnessed the phenomenon admit to being overtaken by an intense feeling of melancholy and sadness. His sorrow is contagious, ensuring that his presence will never be forgotten in Suck Creek.

The Gownsman

Nate Rebhorn was a big believer in allowing fate to take its own course. He believed that everyone followed a path that had been predetermined for them, so it didn't make any sense to waste time mapping out your future or worrying about the consequences of your actions. This strange faith in the inevitability of his own destiny was what led him to concoct extremely odd ways to make his decisions. Since it didn't matter what conclusion he reached—his choices had all already been made by a higher power a long time ago—he felt he should at least have some fun arriving at it.

This was why, when it came time to select a college to attend, he made a list of every decent and semi-decent post-secondary school in the country, tore up the list and put the names into a plastic bag. He then took out the names of 10 schools and applied to all of them. His grades were exceptional and he received invitations to attend all 10 schools, so he pinned their acceptance letters to a large piece of corkboard, covered his eyes with a blindfold and threw a dart blindly into the air. The dart somehow managed to hit the board and impaled itself in the acceptance letter from The University of the South, a school located far away in the town of Sewanee, Tennessee. Nate had never heard of the school or the town, but if that was where fate insisted he was supposed to be, then that was where he was going to go.

Since he had applied to the school without knowing anything about it, he had no idea what to expect when he

The University of the South in Sewanee

got there that September. What he found was a traditional campus, with old buildings that dripped with history and a student body more dedicated to studying than the consumption of anything likely to come out of a keg. All in all it seemed fairly normal, if a bit stuffy, but as he walked across the campus to his dorm room, he did see something that he thought was odd.

While most of the students were dressed in the standard issue clothes found on every campus in North America, there were some who walked around in long black robes, like those he had seen in a movie about an American student who went to school in England. One thing all of the robe wearers seemed to have in common was a certain pride in their steps, an almost arrogant demeanor that suggested they stood above the common fray and could not be bothered by the presence of their fellow students. As soon as he saw them, Nate decided that he didn't like them, but at that point he didn't know why.

When he arrived at his dorm, he discovered that he had been assigned the smallest room on the campus. Instead of grumbling over his misfortune he was delighted to discover that this meant he wouldn't have a roommate, since the tiny room barely had enough space for one bed, much less two. Upon seeing it, he was reminded of his mother's walk-in closet, only without all of the shoes and pantsuits. It contained a small bed, a small desk, a tiny clothes cupboard, a small chair and little else. There was enough room to get from the bed to the desk, and that was about it. Nate imagined that there were felons waiting out the clock on Death Row who had more walking space than he did, but since this apparently was where fate wanted him to live, he shrugged, threw his bags onto the bed and started to unpack.

He quickly ran out of cupboard space and was throwing his socks into one of his desk drawers when someone knocked on his door. He didn't have to go far to answer it. All he had to do was stand up and turn around. Behind the door stood a friendly looking young man his age whose face bore an easy and natural smile.

"Hi neighbor." He stuck out his hand to Nate. "I'm Robert. I'm in the room next door." Robert's voice indicated that he was from a place a lot closer to the college than Nate was. His Southern accent was so thick that it almost sounded like he was faking it.

"Hi Robert." Nate shook his hand. "I'd invite you in, but one of us would have to sit on the bed."

Robert laughed at this like it was the funniest joke he had ever heard. "I'm sorry," he apologized, wiping tears from his eyes, "but I had heard this room was small, but I had no idea until I saw just now."

"So I take it I've scored some well-known digs?"

Robert laughed again and nodded. "My roommate, Farley, was telling me that the students in this dorm have a pool every year over how long it'll take the student who gets this room to run over to the housing office and demand to be moved. He's mad because you lasted more than 10 minutes."

Nate smiled at this. "I hope someone had some cash on me not to show. I kinda like this little space."

"According to Farley, the longest anyone has lasted in here is a week."

"Cool, then that means I get to break a record," Nate answered. "So I take it this Farley guy knows his way around the campus?"

"Yeah, his brother goes here so he knows all of the ins and outs."

"Did he happen to explain why some of the students are walking around in robes?"

"He didn't have to," said Robert. "It's in the school's literature. Didn't you read it?"

Nate didn't think Robert would understand or appreciate the method with which he chose to attend the university so he just shrugged and said, "I guess I must've missed that part."

"It's one of the school's oldest traditions. All students who have earned the school's highest G.P.A.s are allowed to become members of The Order of the Gownsmen."

"So you get good marks and they let you wear a funky robe so everybody knows it?"

"No, it's more than that," Robert explained. "Being a Gownsman—or Gownsperson, I guess—is like being a member of the student government. You can vote on and enact school measures that affect everyone else and not just members of The Order."

"So they get good grades, wear the funky robe and have the power to make decisions that can affect me?"

Robert nodded. "It's all there in the school literature."

"Yeah," Nate sighed, not sure what he got himself into, "I definitely missed that part."

* * *

That night, as Nate attempted to sleep in his small room on his small bed, he found himself dwelling on what he had learned about the Gownsmen at the freshman orientation meeting that he had attended that night with Robert and Farley. Everything Robert had told him had turned out to be true and Nate wasn't sure that he liked it. For some reason he couldn't quite name, he hated the idea that some random keeners who sucked up to the profs during the year were given the right to make decisions that could affect him. From what he heard, The Order hadn't used this privilege of theirs in a significant way for over a decade, but it was more the idea that they could if they wanted to that bugged him the most. It never occurred to him that with his grades and intelligence, he would likely end up a member of The Order by the end of the school year, but then the thought of having to wear that stupid robe would have only depressed him.

After lying in bed for an hour without going to sleep, he opened his eyes, sat up and tried to think of something to do that would help him get some rest. He looked outside his window and decided that a walk would probably do the trick, so he got out of bed, threw his bathrobe over his pajamas and walked out of his room. As he walked past the other rooms he heard other students snoring, talking, laughing, listening to music and arguing. About the only thing he didn't hear come from one of the rooms was silence. As he reached the stairs that led down to the dorm's main lobby, he felt a chill suddenly enter his body, like he had stepped out of a sauna and into a walk-in refrigerator.

"That's a serious freaking draft," he muttered to himself as he made his way down the stairs. As he walked, he noticed an odd thumping noise that seemed to follow him. He turned around and saw that he was still alone, but the sound continued once he started moving again. He didn't know where the noise was coming from, but he reasoned it had to have something to do with how old the stairs were and how they contracted (or something) during the night. The sound stopped once he reached the lobby, which was empty for the first time since he had arrived there that morning. Its silence seemed strange to his ears and made him wonder if there would ever again be a moment when he considered the lack of noise a normal thing, rather than an odd curiosity. He had only been at the university for a day and already he was used to the constant racket that was an unavoidable part of dorm room life.

Outside, the quiet was even more palpable. He was relieved to discover that the silence was making him drowsy and a few more minutes surrounded by it would be enough to help him keep his eyes close once he got back to his bed. As he walked down the steps that led down to the courtyard in front of the dorm building, he was surprised to once again hear the odd thumping noise he'd heard before. This time, instead of a wooden knock, it was a flat thud, which made sense considering that these steps were made out of concrete. Nate turned and once again saw that he was alone, but he lingered in this position longer than he had before since the reoccurrence managed to shatter his previous vague antique construction theory. Now he realized there was no reasonable explanation for the sound and he was starting to get a bit anxious. He then immediately felt stupid for feeling anxious, since the possible supernatural explanation for his anxiety was so completely idiotic it bordered on the insane.

"You're just so tired you're hearing things, buddy," he said to himself. He then realized he was speaking to himself, so he added, "And you're so tired you're getting loopy enough to talk to a crazy person." With that said, he turned around, went back into the lobby, ignored the thumping sound that followed him up the stairs and returned to his tiny room where he immediately fell into a deep sleep.

As he slept, Gerald Pendergast and Peter Deleeuw walked out of the dorm and down the courtyard toward their own residence. Both of them were smiling as they imagined the eventual payoff of the prank they had just set in motion.

Every year two Gownsmen were given the important task of ridding the campus' tiniest room of the ignorant freshman unlucky enough to have had it assigned to him or her. The reason for this yearly eviction was shrouded in the clouds of mystery and time, so much so that even the most knowledgeable members of The Order disagreed on the ritual's true origin. But whatever its initial cause there had yet to be a year when the room hadn't been emptied by the first week of school. In past years the Gownsmen assigned with the task had rid the room of its sole occupant within the first day, but this year, Gerald and Peter had decided to sacrifice speed for the sake of showmanship. This year's eviction was going to be the most extreme in the ritual's history, as they were going to set in motion a series of events that would inevitably lead to the pitiable freshman running screaming out of the room—and quite possibly the campus—forever.

Tonight was the first stage of their conspiracy. Luckily they didn't have to resort to their shaky plan to lure their victim out of his room, as he left it of his own accord. After that it was merely a matter of playing the thumps they had recorded the night before. Wearing their dark robes, they had been able to hide in the dorm's shadows and avoid being seen by their unwitting prey. There was a moment—when he started talking to himself outside the building—when they had to fight to stifle their laughter, but they managed to hold their amusement in and avoid a potential disastrous detection.

"Is everything set for tomorrow?" asked Gerald.

Peter nodded. "I talked to my brother and he knows exactly what to say."

"This," declared Gerald, "is going to be the most memorable prank this campus has seen in a decade."

"No," Peter disagreed, "this is going to be the most memorable pranks this campus has ever seen period."

"You know," noted Gerald, "if this was a cheesy movie, we would be laughing maniacally right now.

"I'm game if you are," said Peter with a grin.

With that, the two of them bwa-ha-ha'ed all the way back to their room.

*　*　*

Nate sat down with Robert and Farley as they all shared their first college breakfast.

"How'd you sleep?" asked Robert. "I couldn't get a wink the entire night."

"I had some trouble at first," answered Nate, "but I eventually managed to crash for a few hours."

Farley looked up from his cereal, which he was spooning eagerly into his mouth. "You didn't hear anything in there, did ya?" he asked as some milk dribbled down his chin.

"Not in my room, I didn't," Nate answered.

"What does that mean?" asked Robert.

"Nothing." Nate shook his head. "It's stupid."

"What isn't?" asked Farley. "What did ya hear?"

"You guys promise you won't think I'm a nut?" Nate leaned in and whispered to them.

"No," they both answered him at the same time. "But we'll listen to what you have to say before we pass our judgment," added Robert.

Nate laughed at this before he continued.

"Last night I decided to go take a walk around the campus and as I was going down the stairs I swore I heard—"

"A strange thumping sound?" Farley interrupted him.

"Yes! So I'm not a nut, and other people have heard it too?"

"Well the jury's still out on that first question, but you're definitely not the first person to hear the sound of The Phantom Gownsman's head going up and down the stairs."

"The Phantom what-now?"

"You haven't heard of The Phantom Gownsman?" Farley asked incredulously.

"No," Nate and Robert answered him at the same time.

"He's the university's most famous legend! How could you two not have heard of him?"

"Give us a break," Nate said. "We haven't any been here two full days."

"No excuse." Farley shook his head. "If there's one thing every student on this campus has to know about, it's The Phantom Gownsman. The consequences of your ignorance could be disastrous."

"So enlighten us, already," Nate grumbled impatiently.

Farley sat up in his seat and looked around the room before he leaned in and began to whisper the way people do when they want to make something sound really dramatic.

"This all happened something like 60 years ago, in the 1940s or thereabouts."

"Hold up," Nate wisecracked, "don't be getting too specific on us."

"Give me a break," Farley said, "it's a legend. Legends aren't supposed to have exact dates. Anyway, there was this guy."

"Does he have a name?" asked Robert.

"What do you want from me? Blood?" asked Farley. "I'm sure he had a name, but I have no idea what it was. I do know he was a seminary student—going to be a priest, y'know? He was the school's top student, so he was a member of The Order."

"A Gownsman?" asked Nate.

"Do we have any other orders here on campus? Yeah, he was a Gownsman, but the rest of The Order wasn't too thrilled about it."

"Why not?" asked Robert.

"Because he wasn't big on the cleanliness. The guy didn't bathe and he never ever washed his robe, so you could literally smell him coming from a mile away."

"You know it's a misuse of the word literally when you use it to back up statements of obvious hyperbole," Robert corrected him.

"Do you want me to tell the story or not?"

"Go ahead."

"Okay. Like I said, the guy smelled so bad you could *figuratively* smell him coming a mile away—"

"That's better."

"And so the rest of the Gownsmen thought he was a major downer for The Order. That was why they eventually started to shun him."

"Shun him?" asked Nate.

"They wouldn't have anything to do with him. He had the highest grades in the school, which meant they couldn't kick him out of The Order, so they just stopped talking to him."

"What did he do?" asked Robert.

"He was so wrapped up in his studies that he didn't even notice. The problem was that, because he was so unhygienic, he started getting this rash across his neck. He was so busy with his work that he didn't notice it, and since no one was talking to him, no one ever mentioned it to him. As the weeks passed it kept getting worse and worse. It started out red, but it eventually started turning green. Occasionally he would find himself scratching at a strange itch on his neck, but he never clued in that he had this long, disgusting, oozing sore forming around his neck. Then one day he just seemed to vanish. He didn't go to any of his classes, and no one saw him at the library he always studied in. Eventually—even though they had shunned him—members of The Order started getting worried that something had happened to him, so they went to his dorm room to find out if he was okay and they were horrified by what they had found."

"What?" Nate and Robert asked together.

"His body slumped over his desk. He had been dead for at least a week, but that wasn't the worst part. When they walked in they saw something weird lying on top of some garbage in his wastepaper basket."

"What was it?" asked Robert.

"It was his head. His rash had gotten so bad and infected that it killed him and as his body sat there slumped on the desk, it continued to fester and rot until finally his lid popped off and rolled into the basket."

"So what does this have to do with the sound that I heard?" asked Nate.

"Well, obviously the guy's spirit wasn't too thrilled with his life turned out, and it was really pissed off at the way The Order shunned him when he was alive, because if just one of his fellow Gownsmen had taken the time to tell him about his rash, he could have gone to a doctor or something. He was also mad because someone stole his head before it could be buried with his body."

"Someone stole his head?" asked Robert.

"According to the legend, yeah."

"Why would they do that?"

"I don't know." Farley shrugged. "People do crazy things. But that's why his headless body can be seen floating around the campus. It's looking for his head."

"And that's what the noise I heard is supposed to be? A ghost looking for his head?" asked Nate.

Farley grinned. "No," he answered, "what you heard was *his head*."

"What?"

"It's true. While his body looks for his head—which is taking a really long time because it doesn't have any eyes or anything—his head is going around campus looking for students it can mess around with. They say it used to only go after Gownsmen, but nowadays it'll go after any- one, regardless of whether they're in The Order or not. That thumping noise you heard? That was The Phantom Gownsman's head following you down the stairs. That's how you know the head is near—by that noise. And you can tell that the body is around when you suddenly become aware of this horrible stink that just comes from out of nowhere."

"People actually believe this?" asked Nate.

"Hey, you heard it yourself last night, but," he leaned in even further, "I haven't even told you the spookiest part."

"What?" asked Nate.

"You know the room where the guy died? You're living in it. Why do you think no one stays there for longer than a week? It isn't because it's so small. It's because The Phantom Gownsman wants it all to himself. I guarantee you, sometime in the next few days, you're going to have more to worry about than a thumping noise following you down the stairs. You're going to see the Gownsman for yourself and you, my friend, are going to freak out!"

* * *

Despite Farley's best efforts, Nate was unmoved by the story of the university's most famous ghost. As he returned to his room after breakfast, he was easily able to logically deconstruct the story in his head until it no longer held up to any rational scrutiny. It was simply a spooky story meant to frighten each year's crop of gullible freshman and he wasn't about to fall for it. Sure, it explained the noises he heard the night before, but that was obviously a deliberate attempt to use an odd quirk of the building to give some small credence to a patently fraudulent story.

And, he decided, even if the impossible was true and the ghost really did exist and covet his bedroom, then it was simply fate, and he'd deal with it as best he could. If, when the time came, he thought the best option was to scream like a little girl and run to the housing department, then that's what he would do, and if he thought he could handle the situation with a bit more aplomb, then that was okay too.

As he prepared for his first class of the semester, Gerald and Peter met with Peter's brother to make sure their plan had been properly set in motion.

"Where's your roommate?" asked Gerald.

"He had a class," answered Farley. "Do you really have to wear those stupid gowns right now?"

"Yes," answered Peter, "we're on official gownsman business. So, what happened during breakfast?"

"I told him the story," Farley shrugged, "but I don't think he bought it."

"It doesn't matter if it believes it or not," Peter told him, "as long as he knows all of the details."

"Did you tell him about the smell?" asked Gerald.

"Yeah," Farley nodded, "I told him everything you guys wanted me to. Personally, I think you guys got a bit unlucky here. Something about this guy tells me he's going to be a tough nut to crack."

"Why do you say that?" asked Peter.

"I don't know," said Farley. "He just has this air about him, like he won't let things freak him out, y'know?"

Peter and Gerald laughed.

"You didn't see him when we played those thumping noises," said Gerald. "He looked pretty freaked out then."

"Okay," said Farley, "but don't say I didn't warn you. Oh, and one more thing."

"What?" asked Peter.

"Where did you get that stupid story about the Phantom Gownsman? I know neither of you are creative enough to come up with that on your own."

"The story of the headless gownsman has been around forever," answered Gerald. "No one really believes it. We just pass it on to scare gullible freshman."

"Gotcha." Farley nodded.

The three of them heard the sound of a door closing to their left.

"That's him," said Peter. "He must be leaving for his first class."

"Perfect!" said Gerald. "We can put Phase II in effect right now."

Farley laughed. "Man, you have no idea how lame that just sounded."

Peter and Gerald ignored him.

"Do you have it on you?" asked Peter.

"It's in my bag," answered Gerald.

"Then let's do this thing!"

The two of them left Farley alone in his room while they walked into the hall and went into Nate's room, using the key The Order had made a decade ago so they could easily pull off the prank year after year.

"Damn!" Gerald swore when the door opened. "I knew this place was small, but I didn't think it would be *this* small."

"I don't think both of us will fit in here," said Peter. "This is going to have to be a one-man operation."

"You stand guard at the door," ordered Gerald. "I'll set up Phase II."

"You know," Peter decided, "it really does sound lame when you talk like that."

"Just stand at the door." Gerald frowned as he closed the door behind him. Alone inside the room, he threw his backpack onto the bed and opened it. He looked inside and found a small jam jar, which he opened very carefully.

"Man, that reeks," he cursed as the odor reached his nose. He placed the open jar on the desk and looked down to the floor below. If Dennis, who pulled off last year's prank, had remembered correctly, then it was the third floorboard from the wall that had been loosened. He bent over and tried to lift it up, and it came up with ease. He turned and grabbed the jar, dropped it into the hidden space in the floor and replaced the board in its proper spot. He closed his bag and left the room. Phase II was now complete, meaning there was only one more phase to go before the most spectacular prank in the university's history would be complete.

* * *

It took Nate exactly one millisecond to notice the very strong smell that had suddenly appeared in his room during the two hours he had been away from it. It was an unpleasant mixture of mildew and body odor, and with his strong nose (his mother was a perfumer and he had inherited her gift of extraordinary olfaction) he was able to determine that it was coming from the floor on the left side of his bed. He sniffed some more. It appeared to be coming from under the third floorboard from the wall. He tried to see if he could lift it up and it came up with ease. He winced as the smell hit him at full velocity and he saw that it was coming from some vile brew that had been mixed together in a small jam jar.

"What the hell?" he muttered as he lifted it out of its hidden crevice.

As he carried it outside and threw it out in the first trash can he came across, he tried to come up with an explanation for why someone would go to the trouble of hiding a jar of stink-juice in his room. The answer seemed pretty obvious to him, so he turned around and headed directly to his dorm room neighbors. He knocked on their door and Farley answered it.

"Hi Nate," he greeted him. "What's going on?"

"You tell me," Nate answered back.

"Pardon me?"

"Who's trying to prank me out of my room?"

"What are you—" Farley started, but it became clear that he didn't have the energy or will to play dumb at that moment. "How did you figure it out?" he asked instead.

"I did the math, and two plus two tends to equal 'let's screw with the freshman.'"

"It's a Gownsman thing. They do it every year. Come in, I'll tell you all about it."

Nate accepted Farley's invitation, walked into his room and listened as his neighbor explained to him who was behind the prank and why.

"Isn't your brother going to be mad that you told me?" Nate asked when Farley finished.

Farley shrugged. "Serves him right for stealing my Halloween candy when I was 11. Y'know," he pondered, "revenge really is sweeter when it's served cold."

"Want to help me get some more of it?" asked Nate.

"Sure. Sounds like fun," Farley smiled.

* * *

"He's really scared," Farley told his brother. "He caught one whiff of that junk you guys threw in there and he came right over and started asking me all of these questions about the Phantom Gownsman."

"Yes!" Peter and Gerald yelled as they pumped their fists and high-fived in rapid succession.

"We got him on the ropes now," Peter said.

"Wait." The joy in Gerald's face vanished suddenly. "You don't think we moved too fast? We might have scared him off before the big finish, and it's nothing without the big finish."

"No," Farley shook his head, "he's still staying in his room. He's acting all brave and said, 'I ain't scared of no ghosts,' or something like that."

"That's a double negative," deduced Peter, "which means he can't be too bright—which means he's going to go down hard!"

"Still," Gerald decided, "we should move quickly, just in case."

"How quickly?" asked Farley.

"Tonight," answered Gerald. "Phase III happens tonight!"

* * *

"So tell me again why I am the one who has to hide under the bed?" asked Peter.

"Don't make me say it," grumbled Gerald.

"I just want to know for sure." Peter grinned.

"You have to hide under the bed because I am too heavy to fit under there," Gerald admitted sourly.

"Too heavy?"

"I'm fat, okay! I can't do it because I'm too fat!"

"Fine, fine. You don't have to get so testy about it. So how are we supposed to get this guy out of his room?"

"Your brother said he was going to handle it."

"I can't believe we're relying on my brother. He's such a wuss. I used to steal his Halloween candy and he never did anything to get back at me for it."

"That's great," mumbled Gerald. "Will you just shut up and keep your eyes on the door. Who knows how long you'll have to sneak into there and get under that bed."

"And why am I the one who has to hide underneath the bed again?"

"I swear I'm going to hurt you when this is through."

"Sheesh, man. Lighten up. This is supposed to be fun."

"It will be when it's over. Wait, Farley is leaving his room, this could be it."

The pair watched as Farley knocked on Nate's door, which opened and revealed their target. He talked to Farley for a minute and then the two of them started down the hall toward the stairway.

"This is it," said Gerald. "Go, go, go. Now!"

Peter ran toward Nate's room and used The Order's key to get inside.

"Wow, it's even smaller when you walk into it," he whispered to himself as he laid down on the floor and shimmied underneath the bed. As thin as he was, it still made for a tight and not very uncomfortable fit.

"Mppffhhhhffff, mppppfffhhhhhh," hissed the walkie-talkie hidden under his robe. He fished it out and talked into it.

"Could you repeat that?" he whispered into the mouthpiece.

"Are you in and under the bed?" asked Gerald.

"Check," he answered. "You really wouldn't be able to fit under here."

"Shut up."

"I'm just teas—"

"No, shut up! They're coming back. We have to end all radio communication."

"What?"

"Turn off your walkie-talkie, nimrod. Man, how the hell did you ever get the grades to make it into The Order?"

"I do well on tests," Peter answered before he turned off his handset and put it back underneath his robe.

The seconds passed very slowly as he lay under the bed. He thought he heard footsteps come from the hallway, but there were so many other sounds inside the dorm it was hard to tell if they were Nate's.

Peter held his breath as he heard what sounded like the twisting of a doorknob. He heard the door to the room open and he saw Nate's feet from underneath the bed. He held his breath and he did his best to not make a sound. Slowly and carefully, he started sliding his head down into the chest of his robe for the proper headless effect, and he was just about to jump out from under the bed when he heard the sound of someone screaming. It was Nate.

But I haven't even jumped out yet, Peter thought to himself, confused by this strange turn of events. He popped his head back out of the robe and watched as Nate's cries caused another set of feet to approach the room's doorway. Peter could tell they belonged to his brother, who, upon seeing whatever it was that Nate saw, started to scream as well.

"What is going on here?" Peter asked, exasperated, as he extricated himself from under the bed. He turned and saw the mangled visage of a 60-year-old decapitated head floating six inches away from his face.

"Aaahhhhhhhhhhhhhhhhhhhhhhhhhhhhhhhhhhhhhhhh hhhh!!!!!!!!!!!!!!!!!" he screamed, before turning around and knocking over both Nate and Farley in his desperate need to escape.

He was halfway down the hall before he heard their laughter.

"What's going on?" asked Gerald, emerging from their hiding space.

"Farley!" swore Peter. "I knew we never should have trusted him!"

The two Gownsmen walked over to the dorm's smallest room and saw its occupant and Peter's brother rolling on the bed, holding their stomachs, giddy with laughter. The floating head was nothing more than a rubber mask stretched over a football and dangled in the air by some fishing line.

"I think we got you guys pretty good," said a voice from behind them. It was Robert.

"Damn it!" Gerald swore as he realized he and his partner were the first Gownsmen to ever fail to pull off The Order's most celebrated annual prank.

"I told you!" shouted Peter. "We should just do it quick and easy like everybody else, but noooooooooooo, you had to be memorable. You had to go for the big score! Now we look like the biggest doofuses on campus!"

At that moment heads started popping out of other rooms as people became curious about the noise. As these students caught on to what was happening, phone calls and emails started to fly. Within a half-hour, everyone on campus knew that Peter and Gerald had messed up The Order's most sacred prank.

They were forced to walk a march of shame as their fellow students left their residences to come out and laugh at their misfortune. Finally, the student body had a reason to feel superior to those arrogant jerks in The Order, and they delighted in Peter and Gerald's misery.

"I'm going to get those guys," Gerald swore angrily when he and Peter finally made it back to their room. "I'm going to teach them the meaning of the word humiliation."

"I don't know," Peter disagreed. "Maybe it would be better if we just let this go."

"Let it go? Let it go?" shouted Gerald. "How can we let this go? They made us look like fools!"

"Well," Peter shrugged, "that's what you get when you try to do something foolish."

"I don't care what you say," Gerald sneered at him. "I am going to have my revenge and it is going to be sweet."

* * *

The following four months passed without incident. People had stopped snickering and whispering behind Peter and Gerald's backs, and Nate had officially blown away the record for longest stay in the campus' smallest room. But during all of that time, Gerald had not stopped seething over the fact that his plan had been so easily foiled, and he still planned to exact some payback on the trio that so thoroughly humiliated him.

He became so obsessed with this new mission that his grades suffered and, as a result, he was forced to leave The Order and return his gown. He no longer cared. His only desire was to see Nate, Farley and Robert become as much of a target for laughter and ridicule as they had made him. It took him some time, but eventually he figured out what he had to do.

* * *

Nate, Robert and Farley had become local campus celebrities after their famous turnaround prank, and as a result found themselves invited to places and parties usually not accessible to freshman. This meant they were away from their rooms a lot, which gave Gerald the opportunities he needed to set up his complicated scheme. After weeks trying to come up with a payback so memorable it would instantly eclipse his own humiliation, Gerald decided to go old school. He was going to do to the trio what angry townsfolk used to do to conmen and swindlers; he was going to tar and feather them.

The first complication in his plan was that there was no way he could use real tar. But after some quick thinking, he concluded that molasses would serve as just a good substitute. In order to sufficiently cover his prey with the sticky substance in an extremely short amount of time, he devised a system in which he submerged a small detonator in a five-gallon jar of the goo and set it off, causing the molasses to explode in all directions. The test result was the messiest thing he had ever seen in his life, and the three mannequins he used as his victims' substitutes ended up covered in the black syrup from head to toe. Then, thanks to a device he had built himself, the sound of the explosion would turn on the industrial fan he purchased at considerable expense. It would blow the large pile of feathers around the room, completely covering Nate, Farley and Robert. It would all happen in less than 15 seconds, so by the time the three of them knew what was happening, it would be too late to do anything about it. At that point, Gerald would set off the dorm's fire alarm and the three of them would be forced to go outside, where they would be seen by everyone.

The plan was so perfect that Gerald could barely stop himself from giggling as he set up his equipment in Robert and Farley's room. The only catch he had yet to work out was how to make sure all three of his targets walked into the room when they got back from whatever party they were currently at. He finally decided that it would be easiest to just put glue in the lock to Nate's door so the freshman would have no choice but to spend the night with his best friends.

As he set up the fan and the feathers in the optimal position, Gerald began to notice an odd smell coming from somewhere inside Farley and Robert's room.

"Man," he choked, "these two really know how to stink up a place."

Assuming that the cause of the smell was most likely an improperly disposed pizza box or a pair of long-unwashed socks, Gerald did his best to ignore the foul odor and kept working on his prank.

* * *

The trouble one so often finds with legends is that they tend not to be as accurate as one would hope. Whether owing to forgetfulness or neglect, unanswered questions or a simple desire to make the tale more entertaining, few tales of local folklore are ever 100 percent accurate. Truthfully, most are barely 25 percent accurate, but as long as they're entertaining, few people seem to mind.

This was not the case with the legend of the Phantom Gownsman. The story that went around campus to scare freshman each year was—most of its tellers would be shocked to discover—89 percent true. One percent of the story's inaccuracy could be attributed to a change in the location of the room in which the Gownsman died. It had not been, as the story insisted, the smallest dorm room on campus, but rather the room next to it. This was a minor detail to be sure, but one that would have been of interest to Gerald at that moment.

Because, as you may have already guessed, the smell that stung his nostrils could not be blamed on any hygienic malfeasance perpetrated by the room's two young occupants. Rather it was the calling card of the ghost whose body had been found in that room over 60 years earlier. The ghost was, as usual, looking for its head (the disappearance of which accounted for the final 10 percent of the story's inaccuracy), and wasn't at all aware of the strange business Gerald was preparing at that moment.

* * *

That night's party proved to be a relatively tame affair, so the three amigos decided to bail on it before it became even more boring. As they walked into their dorm, they heard the sound of a horrible scream followed by a loud explosion and what sounded like an industrial fan. They ran up the stairs to see what was happening and were nearly trampled to death by a terrified, overweight young man covered in what at first glance appeared to be tar and feathers. This feathered fugitive ran screaming down the stairs and straight out the front door. Laughter and catcalls were heard immediately from outside as everyone out on the campus got a good look at this extremely odd sight.

"What was that?" Nate asked, as the three of them tried to comprehend what they had just witnessed.

"I think," Farley said and paused. "I think that was Gerald. Tarred and feathered and screaming like a little girl."

"I think you're right," agreed Robert. "Although based on the smell I'd say it was probably molasses instead of tar."

"Yeah," said Nate, "molasses makes more sense."

The three of them pondered this for a second before running up the stairs to the source of the disturbance. They weren't at surprised to discover that it had happened in Robert and Farley's room.

"Oh my sweet lord," Farley said with some awe as they walked inside and saw that not a single object in the room was not covered with molasses or feathers.

"Wow," said Robert.

"This room," said Nate with a deliberate understatement, "is all kind of messed up."

"And there's Peter," said Farley, pointing to the robed figure in the corner of the room, who managed to convey a sense of powerful shock even though it did not have a head.

Nate stared at person in the robe and came to a very quick conclusion. "I don't think that's your brother, Farley," he whispered out of the corner of this mouth.

The three friends looked at each for clues on what they should do next.

"Isn't this where we run screaming?" asked Robert.

"Wait," Nate said when he saw something strange in the corner of his eye. "What's that?" He pointed to a hole in the wall that had not been there just a few hours earlier. It appeared that the molasses explosion had caused a nearby textbook to slam into the wall hard enough to break the plaster. Even from where the three of them stood, they could see that something was hidden inside the wall. Nate walked over and found out what it was.

"It's a skull," he said, somewhat surprised that he wasn't more shocked by this gruesome discovery.

"Oh my god," said Robert. "Do you know what that is? It's the Gownsman's head!"

"I bet you're right," said Nate as he lifted it out of the wall.

"What are you doing?" asked Farley.

"The poor guy has been looking for this for 60 years. It's about time he got it back," Nate answered as he turned around and approached the headless figure in the corner of the room. "I don't know how it got there, but here it is," he told the Gownsman.

Blindly, the Gownsman held out its hand and Nate handed the spirit the skull. The Gownsman lifted it up and placed it on its neck, where—before their eyes—it began to grow flesh and hair from out of the bone. Within a minute they were looking at a slightly geeky-looking man, only a few years older than themselves.

"Thanks," the man said. "I've been looking for that."

"How did it get there?" asked Farley, trying not to sound as stunned as he felt.

"I don't know." The spirit shrugged. "Probably some stupid prank. I always hated that stuff. Anyway, I've got to go. Thanks for the help and remember if your neck starts feeling really itchy, go and see a doctor."

"Will do," the trio answered together.

The Gownsman then faded out of sight, leaving them alone in the disaster zone that was once Robert and Farley's room.

* * *

No one ever saw Gerald on campus after that. People tried to find out what had happened to him, but he apparently did not want to be found. Peter, who had claimed that his high marks were the result of his being really good at taking tests, was expelled when it turned out that "really good" was his euphemism for "I cheat like crazy." Farley and Robert were given a new room, since it took a full month to clean their old one, which—even years later—never completely lost the smell of molasses. Nate moved too. His tiny room ceased to be charming, and he wanted to be close to his friends. By the end of the year he no longer believed that his fate was predetermined. In an English class he was assigned to read Jean-Paul Sarte's *No Exit* and he decided that he was going to be an existentialist from that point on. Strangely enough this philosophical switchover did very little to change the way he made his decisions, since—either way—it didn't matter where he ended up as long as he had fun when he got there.

The Gownsman was never seen on campus again either. An investigation was organized by the school to uncover how the man's head had ended up inside the wall, but an answer was never found. Like the Gownsman, the investigators finally concluded that it had probably just been the result of some truly bizarre prank, which seemed as good an explanation as any.

An Opry in the Ryman

Some say that music is not created by men, but that it instead rises out of the ground, like a spirit, and takes over the minds of all of those near it who possess the talent to make it heard as something truly magical. For this reason, proponents of that theory claim that certain places at certain times become meccas for musical greatness, attracting all the right musicians to create sonic movements that can still be heard all around the world. Vienna, New Orleans, Liverpool, Detroit and Seattle are just a small handful of places that were once touched by this force, but despite all the great songs and symphonies that came from these spots, none of them have proven influential enough to earn the designation of "Music City."

Say the words "country music" and certain images immediately spring into your mind: cowboy hats and boots, rhinestones and pickup trucks, for example. Depending on your age, you might also think of women with really big hair singing about how they're going to stay with their no good cheatin' husbands because they still love 'em, darn it, or maybe you'll remember when a grizzled old-timer moved you to tears with a song about the girl who broke his heart all those years ago. Younger folks are more likely to recall the genre at its most mainstream, when the line between a country and a pop act was more a matter of attitude and wardrobe than the music itself. But no matter how old you are or where you are from, the words "country music" are instantly synonymous with only one place on earth.

And the reason for this is simple. Nashville is where the Opry is.

Over its 80 years of existence, the Grand Ole Opry has done more for what was once dismissed as "hillbilly music" than any other institution in the world, and in so doing anointed legends whose music remains relevant decades after they played it. In those years it transformed the city of Nashville into the southern version of Hollywood, as thousands of country music hopefuls arrived there each year with dreams of making it big. And for 41 years the temple to which all of these dreamers paid homage was the Ryman Auditorium, the theater that served as home for the Opry. It has seen thousands of dreams realized and shattered, which has definitely taken a toll on the building. It is a haunted place—haunted by those who made it and those who didn't. In it the phantoms of legends commingle with the spirits of failures whose names have long been forgotten, but in truth you'd be hard pressed to tell the difference, because so often the tale of a legend isn't any happier than the story of someone who didn't make it at all.

* * *

The birth of the Opry was as inauspicious as they get. Its first broadcast aired on November 28, 1925, from the fifth floor of Nashville's National Life & Accident Insurance Company building and was hosted by a man named George D. Hay. Only 30 at the time, Hay presented himself as radio's "Solemn Old Judge" and he gave the show several names before—after three years on the air— he dubbed it the "Grand Ole Opry." People from around Nashville clamored to see the show live when it aired and

Grand Ole Opry House in Nashville was a second home to many famous names in country music—along with a few spirits.

soon the small studio on the fifth floor of the insurance building couldn't accommodate the number of people who arrived each week. The show was first moved to the Hillsboro Theatre and then to the Dixie Tabernacle. When the Dixie still proved too small, the show went to the War Memorial Auditorium and started charging a 25-cent admission fee. The logic behind this unprecedented move was that fewer people would be willing to pay to see a show they could hear on the radio for free, but it proved to be a futile effort as the crowds clamoring to see the show only increased. Finally, in 1943—18 years after that first broadcast—the show's producers had no choice but to move the Opry into the largest theater in Nashville.

It makes sense that a place that has housed so many dreams over the decades itself started out as one man's fantasy. Born in 1841, Thomas G. Ryman was a hard-living, hard-drinking man who, thanks to his tenacious business savvy, built what had become the largest steamboat company on the Cumberland River. Over the years he served as captain over his fleet of boats, he developed the reputation of a man who liked to have a good time, and whose idea of a good time always involved a lot of alcohol and a fair share of violence. But his rabble-rousing ways came to an abrupt end when he found himself at a revival meeting led by an itinerant preacher named Samuel Porter Jones.

At this meeting, Ryman was so moved by Porter's words that he decided—right then and there—to forever renounce his hell-raising ways. He vowed to never touch another drop of alcohol and banned all forms of liquor on his boats. He led the life of a pious man but felt that his transformation was not enough to make up for the sins of his wicked past. He decided to build a church that would serve as a home to the evangelist who had changed his life, and also be open to people of every different faith. When it came time to find a site for this church, he chose a spot not far from Nashville's infamous Black Bottoms District. His hope was that men as lost as he was might wander into the church and be graced with the same epiphany that had forever changed his life.

Construction of the Union Gospel Tabernacle finished in 1892 and its doors opened up to a grateful public. It was the largest meeting place in the city and was available not just for church services, but any other public function Ryman deemed appropriate. In 1897 the Tabernacle was made available to a large reunion of Confederate soldiers, but since there were so many of these Rebel veterans, a balcony had to be built to accommodate them. The veterans were only too happy to pay for the project and as a result the balcony was named the Confederate Gallery.

It was here in this balcony that the first of the Ryman's many ghosts was first spotted. A few years after it was built, people began to use the Tabernacle as an entertainment venue as well as a church. Plays, operas, symphonies and concerts were staged in the building and the seats in the Confederate Gallery were cheaper than those on the main floor, which meant that the people who sat there tended to be a bit less "cultured" than the audience below them. As a result, the balcony soon gained a reputation for being a place where a person could have a rowdy good time.

For decades, the spirit of a Confederate soldier has been seen from the gallery during rehearsals.

Sometimes this rowdiness led to violence, but no one knows if it was murder that led to the balcony being haunted by the man in the long gray coat. He is a spirit entirely without a past. No one knows his name or how he came to be there. The color of his coat has led some people to guess that he was once a Confederate soldier and may have been one of the veterans who paid for the balcony's construction, but this theory is no more valid than any other.

He is a quiet ghost and has never spoken to anyone. Instead he has simply allowed himself to be seen countless times over the decades. He is seldom spotted during shows, preferring to instead appear when the theater is nearly empty. During many a rehearsal he has been spotted in the gallery, sitting in a chair that was empty just a second before. At times, production staff who are unfamiliar with the story of his presence have sent people to shoo the spirit away, only to find the balcony clearly empty when they get there. But then, when they get back to the stage, they are shocked to see him sitting in the same spot as before.

* * *

Captain Ryman passed away in 1904, and his memorial service was held in the building his dream had built. Four thousand people gathered to remember him, and it was decided that a man so beloved should be honored in a way that long preserved his memory. To this end the Union Gospel Tabernacle was renamed the Ryman Auditorium, and it became evident that the captain was so touched by this gesture that his spirit decided to linger in the building that bore his name.

Though no one has claimed to have ever seen the captain's ghost, that hasn't stopped his spirit from making its presence felt. Over the century that passed after his death, there have been several events staged at the auditorium that would not have met with his approval had they been presented while he was alive. Whether this was because they were too risqué, possibly blasphemous or contrary to his politics, they would have all made him uncomfortable, and his spirit has no qualms expressing that fact.

Several productions and concerts at the Ryman have found themselves the victims of unexplainable sabotages. Stage lights burn out at the worst possible moments, curtains close when they shouldn't, performers are struck suddenly mute on stage, scenery collapses and instruments inexplicably go out of tune during the middle of a musical number. While some of these incidents have been explained with more rational explanations, many people believe they are directly attributable to the captain's displeasure with the performance at hand. And when even these tricks have failed to make the proper impression, the captain's spirit has been known to make such a racket during the performance of these productions that audiences have actually demanded their money back, since they were unable to hear what was happening on stage.

That's not to say that the captain's ghost is always a grumpy sort of spirit, as it has been known to show signs of a slightly devious sense of humor over the years. The most famous example of this occurred when a television crew from New York City arrived at the theater to film a special for one of the networks. When the filming was complete, members of the TV crew spoke with the Ryman's regular staff, who told the New Yorkers several stories about the theater's namesake phantom.

The television folks considered themselves to be intelligent, sophisticated people, and they listened to the stories of the late captain's exploits with obvious disbelief, making sure to ask extremely patronizing questions that only served to mock their storytellers' sincerity. But the local staff remained unperturbed by the TV crew's rudeness. They suggested that if the crew didn't believe them, maybe they should stay a little while longer and find out for themselves that the captain's ghost was no idle fantasy.

The TV crew decided to call the theater staff's bluff and delayed their plans to return to New York right away. They hunkered in for a long night at the auditorium, just to prove that they weren't going to be fooled by a bunch of Tennessee rubes.

When it became clear that the crew wasn't going anywhere, the theater staff started to grow worried. There was no guarantee that the captain's ghost would do anything to make his presence known that night, and if he didn't they would look just like the fools the New Yorkers thought they were.

They decided that the only thing they could do was fake a paranormal incident and hope that their trickery wasn't obvious. But this was easier said than done. As the hours passed the staff tried to think of just one thing they could do that would scare the pants off the New Yorkers. Suddenly, one of them got an idea.

"I know where the Opry folks keep the sound effects equipment they sometimes use on their radio broadcasts. They have this device that creates the sound of really heavy footsteps. I could take it and sneak around the auditorium and make it sound like some invisible person is walking around the theater!"

Everyone thought this was a great idea, so the fellow who proposed it ran off to find this piece of equipment, while the others waited to see how these strange sounds would affect the blasé TV folks. A few minutes later, just as the clock struck midnight, the sounds of very heavy footsteps echoed throughout the auditorium. The local staff watched with glee as the TV people started to become unnerved by these seemingly unexplainable noises.

"Look at that!" One of the New Yorkers pointed up toward the bottom of the balcony. At the sound of each footstep, the dust gathered between the crevices of the ceiling panels fell onto the seats below.

This eerie sight was enough to spook the skeptics and they hightailed it out of the theater back to New York.

When they were gone, the local staff congratulated themselves on putting one over on the snide big-city types. They were soon joined by the perpetrator of the prank, who was immediately complimented for his work.

"What are you talking about?" he asked them. "I just spent the last half-hour trying to get that stupid footstep device, but I couldn't find it anywhere. Hey," he turned and looked around, "what happened to those TV folks? Did something happen while I was gone?"

He could tell by the stunned expressions on his co-workers' faces that something had happened and that if he hadn't done it, then someone—or more accurately *something*—else had.

* * *

During the four decades that the Ryman served as the home of the Opry, it was a second home for many of the most famous names in all of country music. Many, if not all, of the country music singers who are considered legends today got their start on that very stage, but out of them all, one figure stands alone. Both as a singer and a songwriter, this Opry star set the standard for what was considered country music genius, and as big as his impact was on the genre, it might have even been bigger if he hadn't died at such a young age.

Hank Williams was 24 the first time he played at the Opry. It was 1949, six years after the show had moved to the Ryman. A skinny, frail-looking young man, Williams had suffered from spinal bifida when he was a boy. The condition had taught him how painful life could be at a very early age, and he had chosen to take the harsh lessons he had learned and transform them into songs he played on his guitar. At first, Williams had taken to playing music as his hobby because he couldn't play sports, but soon he became so good at writing songs that it seemed possible he could make a living at it.

In the beginning Williams found that breaking into show business was nearly impossible, especially for someone who looked and sounded like he did. Music publishers instantly recognized his talent as a songwriter, but record labels were a lot less kind. He sang his songs with a nasal twang that—to some ears—sounded more like the cry of an animal than the kind of voice people expected to hear on the radio, but eventually he was able to get a deal with MGM Records in 1947.

Over the next two years he released a series of singles that managed to get him noticed by both the industry and the general public. His sound was a divisive force; people either loved him or hated him—ambivalence was not an option. But the nature of that sound—that cry that reminded some of a wounded beast wracked in agonizing pain—was not an affectation. Williams truly was a wounded soul, his own worst enemy. He arrived at his concerts too drunk to perform and treated everyone around him with the worst kind of contempt. His first wife, Audrey, told him that she wanted a divorce. For a time it seemed like his career would end before it had even truly begun, but then he wrote the song that would make him a star.

His producers considered "Lovesick Blues" a throwaway—a song not even worthy to serve as the B-side to his latest single, but Williams believed it was possessed by something special, and he was right. The song went straight to number one on the country charts, and soon he got the call to appear at the Opry.

At once he went from being a regional curiosity to a national sensation. His songs touched a chord with people that no other country music performer had ever been able to reach, but his demons would not allow him to enjoy his success. Just three years later he was fired from the Opry for his unprofessional behavior and Audrey finally made good on her threat to divorce him. He married again, a pretty young girl named Billie Jean, but it made little difference in his behavior. He was on a downward spiral that was suddenly cut short by the car accident that took his life. It happened sometime after midnight on the first day of 1953. He was just 29.

That year, three more of his songs hit the charts and his legend began to grow. His influence appeared in the way other country artists wrote their songs and how they sang them; it even went beyond the "hillbilly music" for which he was famous. Bob Dylan would later admit that Williams was an important influence on him as a musician, and it could be argued that people were more willing to accept Dylan's unique vocal sound because of the path Williams had previously set.

Of all the many performers who would have cause to haunt the Ryman Auditorium, Williams is the one whose presence there makes the most sense. His was a talent that made him a legend, at the cost of his own happiness.

He had known the glory of performing in the most famous country-western show in the world, but didn't care for it enough to change his self-destructive ways. Such a legacy would lead anyone to be devoured by regret, and regret is what brings so many spirits back to this world.

Not long after Williams died, an Opry singer named Whispering Bill Anderson was performing a sound check for that evening's show. Almost without thinking about it he started to play one of William's favorite songs. Something about the way he played it caused everyone around him to stop and listen to the pretty tune. Midway through the song, the sound cut out and the whole theater plunged into total darkness. When the lights finally came back on, an electrician was called to find out the cause of this sudden blackout, but no reasonable explanation could be found. Anderson later insisted that the moment was one of the eeriest he had experienced in his entire life and that it was somehow related to the playing of that particular song.

Some time later—nearly 20 years after the Opry left the Ryman for its own theater on the outskirts of Nashville—a construction worker had a much closer encounter with the spirit of this country music legend when the auditorium was closed for some necessary renovations. So caught up in his work, the man failed to notice that everyone else had gone home for the night. When he tried to leave himself, he discovered to his chagrin that he was locked inside. He couldn't find a phone that worked and had resigned himself to spending the night in the building when he heard the sound of a guitar playing on the stage. He followed the sound of the music and was shocked to see a skinny-looking man on stage.

"How'd you get in here?" he asked the man, but before the stranger could say anything he vanished right in front of the man's eyes.

The man was so frightened by this that he grabbed a nearby sledgehammer and used it to break a window so he could escape from the theater. At first he was uncertain who the ghostly stranger had been, but then he saw a photograph of Williams and instantly identified him as the spirit he had seen that night.

* * *

How many more ghosts haunt the Ryman Auditorium? It's impossible to say. Few have ever made their presence as powerfully felt as the three spirits mentioned above, but that does not mean they are not there. If ever there was a place that was meant to be haunted it would have to be this theater, which has seen so much greatness on its stage over the course of the 11 decades it has existed. Not only is it a monument to the generosity of the man who built it, but it is also a monument to the influence that the city of Nashville, Tennessee has had on the entire world.

Thanks to a great tradition that first started on the fifth floor of an insurance company building 80 years ago, "Music City" is more than a place where people go to become country music stars. It's a place where one can actually come face to face with the spirits of legends.

Ladies and Gentlemen, The King Has Not Left the Building

If there was ever a contest held by all 50 states to determine which one has had the greatest impact on the world, Tennessee would place much higher than most people watching this pageant might at first assume. Sure, California and New York would probably take the top spots, but the representatives of the Volunteer State would simply have to say one name to clinch the bronze.

"Ladies and gentlemen," they would announce into the microphone, "Elvis Aaron Presley."

This extraordinary man raised throughout his teens in Memphis had a talent and a charisma that took him from being a truck driver to a teen idol to a movie star to an icon recognized by men and women who have never even heard of the state he came from. But he not only entertained, he changed the world. The uninhibited rebellion evoked by the infamous gyration of his hips started an earthquake that transformed the repressed conformity of the 1950s into the brash individualism of the 1960s. As the man who turned the hard-pounding outlaw rhythms of rock and roll into a sound embraced by a mainstream audience that previously considered such milquetoasts as Pat Boone and Perry Como the top of the musical heap, he made being young seem as cool as it could ever possibly be.

The girls had screamed for Frank Sinatra, but not like they screamed for Elvis. Those young ladies, all on the verge of womanhood, shouted and cried with the fervor of those who had undergone a transformative religious epiphany. As they would with a group of four young lads from Liverpool, England, they shouted so loudly as he performed that they could not even hear him sing. This was a shame because his was a voice that—if his most ardent admirers are to be believed—could literally work miracles.

It was a deep, confident voice, softened by the upbringing of a loving mother who taught her son to always be respectful and polite. But with his hair styled like his favorite comic book hero, Captain Marvel Jr., and a perpetual sneer plastered on his face whenever he stood in front of a TV camera, it's no wonder so many parents were concerned about the effect he was having on their children. He looked dangerous. He played dangerous music. And the way he moved those hips!

They tried to stop him any way they could. Some burned his records in bonfires. TV execs ordered that he only be filmed from the waist up. And then, just as they would years later with another great American icon, Muhammad Ali, they drafted him into the army. None of it worked. He only became a bigger star. After the army, he became an actor and appeared in a string of some of the worst movies Hollywood ever made. For every classic like *Jailhouse Rock*, *Viva Las Vegas* and *Love Me Tender* there were 10 turkeys with titles like *Harum Scarum*, *Kissin' Cousins*, *Clambake* and (worst of all) *A Change of Habit*.

They were all hits, all of them. And their soundtracks made millions.

In 1968 he gave up on the movies and started singing again. Even in the age of Woodstock and the Summer of Love, his television comeback special was a major cultural event. Compared to the other musicians of that time, he no longer seemed as dangerous as he had 15 years earlier, but there was no denying he was still the king. And every king needs a castle to rest in. Elvis called his Graceland.

He bought the mansion in 1957 for $102,500 from a Memphis socialite named Ruth Brown Moore, while on a break from filming *Loving You*, his second movie for Paramount Studios. The then-10,000 square-foot mansion was built out of tan Tennessee limestone, and Elvis quickly made it his own by adding over 7000 feet of space, as well as a gate that surrounded the 13.7 acre estate, which—in a nod to its owner's first artistic profession—was decorated by several hundred musical notes.

Ten years later, Graceland was finally graced by the presence of a queen when Elvis married Priscilla Beaulieu, a beautiful brunette who was envied, hated and adored by hundreds of thousands of women around the world. The next year saw the birth of Graceland's only princess, Lisa Marie, who would grow up to inherit her mom's beauty and her father's charismatic sneer. But this fairytale did not last. In 1973, Priscilla and Elvis divorced. Decades of adoration and worship had taken a serious toll on Elvis. Unable to handle the pressures of being the world's most famous singer, he turned to drugs and food for comfort.

His infamous diet, which consisted of such dishes as the Fool's Gold Loaf (bake one whole baguette slathered

Is it the ghost of Elvis or just one of his many impersonators who has been spotted at Graceland?

with butter, then cut it in half, scoop out the insides and insert one pound of crisp bacon and one jar each of peanut butter and grape jelly, press the two halves together into a sandwich and serve to a person who no

longer cares about anything), caused his weight to balloon. The times started changing and he soon seemed like
a cultural dinosaur, an act whose time had come and
gone. He played in Vegas, where he could at times be as
brilliant as he had ever been or just as easily slip into a
state of unconscious self-parody, sweating and karate
kicking in front of audiences too square to realize their
hero was no longer cool.

Elvis lived surrounded by sycophants who depended
on him to make a living and who refused to acknowledge
that he was inevitably spiraling toward an early death. It
finally happened in 1977, when he had a heart attack in
his private bathroom in Graceland. He was 42 years old.

As news of his death spread around the world, people
forgot the man who had in the past few years devolved
into a caricature of himself, and instead remembered the
icon who had changed the world. Like Mick Jagger once
sang, we didn't know what we had until it was gone.
People from all over the planet came to Graceland to
mourn Elvis' passing. Some took it even further and did
their best to become him. Elvis impersonators had been
around while he was still alive (it has been reported that
the late comedian Andy Kaufman was his favorite), but
the news of his death caused hundreds, if not thousands,
of men (and a few women) to come out of the closet and
embrace their inner-king. Ironically, most of them honored their hero by impersonating who he was during the
period of his personal nadir, if only because it was a lot
easier for most men to pretend to be the overweight Elvis
of the 70s than the handsome idol of the 50s and 60s.

In the 80s this adoration took on an almost religious fervor. People refused to believe that he was really dead and books were written that explained how he had faked his death to get out of the limelight. The authors of these books appeared on talk shows and told of personal encounters they had had with the still-living king. But it was merely a way for some unethical men and women to eke out a living by allowing thousands of people the false hope that their hero was still alive and may yet return.

The king was really dead, and this was evident in the home he had lived in for 20 years. This proof isn't found in the monument that marked his grave, which rested behind the mansion on Graceland's estate, but rather in the spirit that has lingered in the house for three decades following his death.

There have been countless sightings of Elvis' ghost but, considering the fanaticism and devotion of his most ardent fans, this was entirely expected. In the same way that an extremely devout Catholic is much more likely to see the image of the Virgin Mary on a burnt piece of toast than someone who hasn't been in a church in years, true Elvis acolytes are much more likely to report having seen the ghost of their idol than someone who has no idea what lies down at the end of Lonely Street (answer: Heartbreak Hotel). It is because of this fact that so many of these reports can be quickly and easily dismissed, as they serve much the same role as the rumor that Elvis is still alive after having faked his death.

But while this is true for most ghostly Elvis sightings, there are, of course, exceptions. Not everyone who has visited Graceland is a fan of the man who made it famous.

Some are dragged there by others and have no interest in taking the popular tour through Elvis' home. Some are there for professional reasons, such as to take photographs for a newspaper or conduct interviews with the mansion's staff and visitors. Some go there because, just like the Empire State Building in New York or the Eiffel Tower in Paris, it's the kind of landmark one visits simply because it's there and a trip to the city wouldn't be complete without seeing it up close. These people's perceptions have not been clouded by their adoration for the dead superstar. They can see beyond their feelings for him and admit that his taste in home décor erred on the wrong side of tacky and that the interior of the famous mansion serves as a monument to everything that was wrong with the popular styles of the 1970s. If to some, Graceland has the aura of a church, then the aforementioned visitors are the non-believers and their stories of contact with the spirit of the king are much harder to deny.

When Betty Hollend (not her real name) first walked into Graceland she found it extremely difficult to stop herself from giggling. She was 16 and was only there because her parents, both huge Elvis fans, decided to come to Memphis that year specifically just to see their favorite performer's home. Like all 16-year-olds she thought her parents were the very definition of the word lame and felt an instinctual compulsion to reject anything they took pleasure in, which meant that she thought anything related to Elvis was a joke. The other tourists around her didn't help matters, as most of them—to her eyes—dressed and acted exactly like her parents.

She turned out to be the only teenager in the tour group and dealt with disapproving looks as she laughed at some of the more atrocious design elements they came across in the house. This got old very quickly, so she decided to sneak away from the group and do some exploring on her own. She was only away from the group for a few minutes before she realized that she had to pee. She found a bathroom that she could tell wasn't meant for the tourists, but since no one was around she decided to go in it anyway.

She took care of her bladder's pressing need and washed her hands in the sink. While cleaning her hands she caught sight of a strange reflection in the mirror in front of her. She looked up and saw a man dressed like Elvis standing behind her.

"I'm sorry," she apologized, "I really had—"

But before she could explain any further the man behind her disappeared.

Betty ran out of the bathroom and rejoined the tour. Her parents asked her what was wrong, but she didn't want to tell them what she had just seen. The tour continued and she soon learned that the bathroom she had been in was the site of Elvis' fatal heart attack. She then told everyone of her strange encounter with the ghost of a legend.

Another bizarre incident occurred a short time later when a photographer from a well-known magazine was sent to take pictures of the mansion for an article commemorating the anniversary of Elvis' death. Like Betty, he was not a fan of the singer and was openly scornful of the place and the people who had come from all around the world to see it. He spent a few hours getting the shots he needed before he went back to his home in New York. There he started developing the pictures, but was shocked to discover that not a single one of them was any good. They were all out of focus or overexposed, which had never happened to him before in his entire professional life. But what really spooked him was the last photograph he developed. It was blurry like all of the others, but in the corner of the frame he saw a shadowy face that he found instantly familiar thanks to the king's famous raised upper lip.

At first the photographer was worried because he had failed to get the shots he needed for the assignment, but he then realized that a photograph of the ghost of Elvis was worth 10 times as much money as the magazine was going to pay him for the pictures they had wanted. But before he could sell the picture, the negative was destroyed in a freak accident. He still had the original photo, which he showed to several people, but before he could sell it, it was also destroyed when a hot ash from his cigarette fell on it and caused it to ignite.

A few years after this incident members of a now-defunct punk-rock band called The Crooked Straights stopped into Memphis during what would be their first and only attempt at a tour. With all four members and their soundman crammed in with all of their equipment in one van, their nerves frayed very quickly and they became extremely tense with each other. Only a dozen people showed up to their gig in Nashville, in the most run-down, depressing bar they had ever seen. Needing some kind of relief from their misery, they decided to visit Graceland. None of them were actually fans of Elvis.

In fact, they hated what he had come to represent and were openly contemptuous of anyone who thought otherwise, but they were pretty sure that a few hours spent in the man's house, surrounded by his fans, would yield at least a few much-needed laughs.

They hadn't even walked through the front entrance before they started laughing at the people around them. They tried their best not to be too rude, since they didn't want to get kicked out, but given how absurd they found the place, it took a lot of effort on their parts. They giggled and guffawed their way through the tour, annoying most of the other tourists, who didn't see what was so funny about the home of the world's greatest entertainer.

Of all the sights they saw that day, the one they found the funniest was Elvis' TV room with its famous row of television sets that allowed the king to watch what was on every channel at once. The five punk rockers laughed as they recalled stories they had heard about Elvis shooting at the TV sets whenever they showed something he took exception to. The tour continued, but the five of them lingered in the TV room, too amused by its tacky extravagance to leave it.

"I heard he shot one of these things every time he saw Robert Goulet," the group's singer told the others.

"Wow," said the drummer, "me and Elvis have something in common."

"Who's Robert Goulet?" asked the bassist.

"Another really cheesy singer," answered the soundman. "You know, I bet this would be easier than flipping through all the channels," he admitted.

"Yeah," agreed the lead guitarist, "but nowadays you need a lot more sets than this."

The group's singer was about to say something to this when one of sets suddenly turned on. The sound of white noise hissed as static played on its screen.

"Did one of you guys do that?" he asked the others.

"No," they all answered at once.

Then another set turned on, then another and another. Soon all of the sets were broadcasting the same static filled image. The soundman walked over to one and tried to turn it off, but when he twisted the dial, it did not respond and kept hissing out white noise with the others. He tried to turn off all the other sets, but they too refused to be switched off.

None of them were laughing anymore. The volume of the sets grew louder and louder and just as they were forced to cover their ears they heard something in the static that sounded like a very famous voice.

"Get out of my house," it said very calmly.

With that, all of the TV sets turned off and the five men ran out of the mansion and back into their van. Their tour ended a week later and they broke up not long after that.

Now these are just three cases out of the hundreds in which people have claimed to see the ghost of Elvis Presley. There is no way to know which of these sightings were genuine and which ones were not, and it is possible that these three do fall into that other category, but they are interesting in that they all involve people who had no emotional investment in seeing the ghost that many people believe haunts Graceland.

And then again, to acknowledge all of the possibilities, I admit that I could be wrong and that all of those people who claim the King of Rock & Roll is still alive are right. Maybe none of the Elvis ghost stories are true because the man is still out there enjoying his well-deserved retirement, but I sincerely doubt it. If Elvis were still alive, I really think he would have come out of hiding when Lisa Marie married Michael Jackson.

2
Legends

For the Love of Nocatula

In John's dream, he was not yet dead. He had—despite the presence of an unwelcome piece of steel buried somewhere inside his chest—somehow survived the long hour of battle he and his fellow loyalists had lost on the King's Mountain. In this dream he had found the strength to stagger off the bloody field and escape into the nearby woods. There, in the wilderness, his dream lost all sense of time and he wandered for what felt like days but could just have easily been minutes or hours. Finally, he collapsed, and for a time, his dream faded into a darkness that was only occasionally relieved by random moments of sensation, be it a sound, a smell or the sight of the tree beside him. Lying there, he became aware that the dream was close to ending and he prayed that when it did, he would not be unwelcome in the world he imagined lay beyond it.

But before the dream could end and the darkness around him solidified into an impassable barrier, John felt one last powerful jolt of sensation that—for a moment—made him wonder how a dream could ever feel so real. It began with the sound of light footsteps slowly moving toward him. It continued with the smell of something soft and delicate yet distinctly human—a combination of flowers and perspiration—and it ended with the sight of a beautiful woman kneeling overtop of him. Her hair was long and dark and her skin was tanned. She looked down at him with large brown eyes and spoke to him in a language he did not understand. Seeing her made him smile

In the wilderness, his dream lost all sense of time...then a beautiful angel appeared.

because it was clear to him that the dream was finally over and he was being greeted by an angel.

"I'm ready," he whispered to her. "Take me to wherever I belong."

She did not seem to understand him, and instead of taking him to his eternal reward, she bade him to be silent and turned and shouted out into the woods. Her words were met with the sound of hurried footsteps and John saw more angels—some men, some women. He became confused when the darkness he thought he had left forever began to surround him once again. Slowly it consumed all he saw around him and as the angels surrounded him where he lay, his dream came to an end.

* * *

John awoke with a start. He tried to sit up, but a sudden shot of pain in his chest stopped him cold. It was dark, but there was enough light coming from outside that he could see that he was in a small wooden hut. It took him a moment to put the pieces together and realize that he was not dead and that his experience in the woods had not been a dream. The men and women he had seen standing around him had not been angels, but were the people who had walked this land long before any European had ever considered its existence. But before he could do anything with this knowledge, he fell back into unconsciousness; his wound left him little strength to stay awake for more than a few minutes.

The next time he awoke, he could feel the sensation of water in his mouth. When he opened his eyes, he saw the same beautiful face of the woman in the woods.

"Thank you," he said weakly. Though she did not speak English, he could tell that she understood when she smiled at him.

Days passed by and John slowly began to regain his strength. During his convalescence, the only person he saw was the beautiful woman who had never so much as told him her name. With every moment that he spent with her, it became clearer to him that his initial belief that she was an angel wasn't far from the truth. For a reason he could not fathom, this stranger who owed him nothing had dedicated herself to making sure that he would live, and he soon decided that her kindness should not go unrewarded. He became more and more determined to get well, if only so he could get the chance to return his gratitude.

After what felt like a month, he was finally visited by someone other than his angelic caretaker. It was a man, strong and tall, with the same features as John's kind nurse.

"Parlez-vous français?" asked the man, his accent perfect.

John shook his head. He couldn't speak French.

"Then you are English," he said.

"That's right," John said and nodded, surprised to hear his language from one of the Natives' lips.

"I am fearful that my English is not as well as my French," the man admitted. "I speak it fine enough to get by. I have been wishing to speak to you for some time, but my daughter did not want you to have any visitors until she thought you were able."

"Your daughter?" asked John.

"Yes, Nocatula Cooweena. She has been the one caring for you these past days."

"Nocatula…" John said to himself. He was grateful to finally know his angel's name, which—he decided—was as beautiful as she was.

"I am Attakulla-kulla," the man told John. "What am I to call you?"

John introduced himself.

"Well, John, you are welcome to stay here for as long as you need. But I warn you, I would not try to leave before my daughter says you can go. She can be as stubborn as she is beautiful."

John thanked him for his hospitality.

"It is our way," Attakulla-kulla explained. "Now I shall go and let you rest."

"Wait." John tried to sit up before the pain in his chest stopped him.

"What is it?" asked Attakulla-kulla.

"You are good with languages?" asked John.

"It is a skill I have been gifted with," Attakulla-kulla answered.

"Do you think you could teach me your language?"

Attakulla-kulla laughed. "You want to speak to her, don't you?"

"Yes."

"Then I shall teach you."

* * *

A few weeks later, Nocatula walked into the hut and found John sitting up with an odd smile on his face. She had never seen him look so happy before.

"Hello Nocatula," he greeted her in her language.

"What did you say?" she asked him, not sure if she should believe her ears.

John laughed at her amazement. "I can say more than that," he told her.

"How?"

"Your father has been teaching me. I asked him not to tell you. I wanted to surprise you."

She still looked stunned. "How long has he been doing this?"

"Since the day you first let him visit me."

"But how could you learn so much so fast?"

"I am quick learner and your father is a very good teacher."

"I cannot believe it."

"Why? Did you think your patient was an oaf?"

"No," she said and laughed. "It is just that I had hoped that we could someday speak, but I never dared think it would happen this soon."

"What did you want to talk about?" he asked.

Nocatula blushed. "Nothing important," she admitted.

John smiled. "Thanks to your father's patience and kindness, we can talk about nothing important all day long. He is a very good man."

"Yes," she said. "I stand here as proof of his virtues."

Then she sat down beside him and grabbed his hand and told him the tale of how she would not exist were it not for the mercy of her father.

"When the English started coming to this land, my father treated them with great respect, but this respect was not reciprocated and he was often treated as a fool and betrayed by those who were once allies. Finally, when it proved more than his pride could bear, he declared war on the colonists and laid siege on a settlement called Fort Loudon. The people in the fort were trapped there for months and ran out of food and water. When starvation weakened them, they surrendered. Since the colonists had not honored their oaths to the Cherokee, many of our braves decided that there was no reason for us to honor our oath to them, so they began to attack the men and women who were too weak to fight back. My father could not stop them, but when a fleeing woman with her baby son in her arms fell at his feet, he took mercy on her and told her that they would have his protection and come to no harm. It was then that a brave named Mocking Crow came upon them and tried to attack the woman and her baby. My father ordered him to stop, but Mocking Crow was filled with a horrible lust for blood and ignored his chief's commands. He lunged at the woman and my father killed him with a single blow. He then took her back to our village and made her his wife and her child, his son, and together they had me, Nocatula."

"That is a good story except for the part where all those people get killed," he told her.

"Sometimes I think I should leave that part out, but I can't," she said sadly.

"Tell me, Nocatula, how soon will it be until I am strong enough to go outside?"

"A matter of weeks. Why?"

"Because when I do, I want to make sure I am strong enough to prove to your father that I am worthy to be your husband."

She smiled. "I think that you may have already done that."

* * *

As John rested, Nocatula left him alone so she could thank her father for the wonderful gift he had given to her. She was close to his home when she was stopped by a voice so irritating that a person risked madness listening to it.

"How is your white man today?" asked the voice.

"He is well, Mocking Crow," she answered curtly.

The story she had told John had not been a lie, as the man now talking to her was the son of the brave killed by her father that day. When he reached manhood, he had taken his father's name, both to honor him and to show that he had no respect for the man his tribe called their chief. But his hatred for Attakulla-kulla was not transferred to the chief's daughter, whom Mocking Crow had loved since she was a young girl. Nocatula never once reciprocated his feelings. She had instead always made it clear that she did not like the abrasive and irritating man and merely being near him was enough to make her itch. Unfortunately for her, Mocking Crow was as stubborn and clueless as he was grating on the nerves, and it was obvious to everyone that he would do anything to ensure that she would be his wife someday.

"I would have left him to die in the woods," said Mocking Crow.

"You have never had a generous heart," she retorted.

"What has he done to deserve our kindness and mercy?"

"Our kindness and mercy, Mocking Crow? I was not aware you had showed him such sentiments."

"What has he done to deserve all of your time caring for him?" he asked.

"He has done nothing, but what kind of person would I be if I helped only those who had earned my attention?"

"A smart one," he answered.

"As always it has been a pleasure talking to you, Mocking Crow, but I must go see my father."

"Are you going to tell him stories about your white man?"

"Yes, among other things," she told him before walking away.

* * *

Within a month, John was strong enough to walk and go outside. Once again he proved himself a quick learner, picking up the ways of Cherokee life as quickly as he did the language. He was immediately accepted and well liked by the tribe. The only people who treated him like an out-sider were Mocking Crow and his friends, who made it clear from the beginning that there was nothing John could do that would convince them that the Englishman was worthy of being a member of their tribe.

The more time John and Nocatula spent together, the more obvious it became to everyone that they were in love. It simply became a matter of time before he would ask her father for his permission to marry her. And when he finally did, Chief Attakulla-kulla was only too happy to give his blessing.

Mocking Crow was outraged and he told the chief that there would be serious consequences if he allowed this marriage to continue. His boldness enraged Attakulla-kulla, who ordered that the jealous suitor be banished from the tribe. Mocking Crow left the village, but he was not alone. His friends left with him, vowing that they would soon return to take vengeance on their foolish chief.

When the dust from this unpleasantness settled, John and Nocatula were married. As part of the ceremony, John was given the Cherokee name Connestoga and made an official member of the tribe. The two of them lived as man and wife for two weeks before fate decided it was time that their happiness end.

Connestoga was out in the woods, hunting for food, when he found himself surrounded by Mocking Crow and his men. He tried to fight them, but they grabbed him and took him back to the camp they had established fol-lowing their exile. He was tied up and left there alone for several hours. He had no idea what was happening, until he heard the sound of a woman screaming and crying in the distance.

"Nocatula!" he shouted, recognizing the cries as those of his wife.

He heard her shout back in the distance. "Connestoga!"

Within minutes, Mocking Crow and his men returned with a weeping Nocatula. With a knife in his hand he walked over to her helpless husband with a wicked smile on his face.

"You think this white man is worthy of your love?" said Mocking Crow. "Well, let's see how worthy he is with my knife in his belly!"

"No!" Nocatula cried out, but there was nothing she or her husband could do. Mocking Crow lifted up his blade and stabbed it deeply into Connestoga's stomach. For his part, Nocatula's husband did not give Mocking Crow the satisfaction of a scream of pain. As the knife twisted in him, he did nothing but stare at his murderer with pure hatred in his eyes.

With his very last breath, he said to Mocking Crow, "You may have killed me, but you will never know her love, and you will never have a moment's peace for as long as you shall live."

Mocking Crow just laughed and stabbed Connestoga again and again, until he was certain that the man was dead.

Nocatula sobbed uncontrollably as her beloved lay lifeless on the ground in front of her. She was silenced only when Mocking Crow walked over to her and slapped her to the ground.

"Do not waste your tears on that dog," said Mocking Crow. "This is the happiest day of your life. It is the day you get to be wife of a true Cherokee brave."

"Never!" she yelled.

"You are angry now, but soon you will see that this is the way it should have always have been, were it not for the foolishness of your addle-minded father. Now stand up, it is time for us to be married."

With this, his men lifted her to her feet and untied her hands. As soon as her hands were free from her bonds, she lunged at Mocking Crow and wrestled his bloody knife from out of his hands.

"You may kill one of us, but you cannot kill us all!" said Mocking Crow.

She spoke sadly with the knife shaking in her hand. "You always were a fool. I have no intention of killing any of you."

She then raised the blade and plunged it into her own heart.

* * *

Mocking Crow and his men were long gone by the time the bodies of Nocatula and Connestoga were finally found. A search party had been formed as soon as it had become clear that the couple was missing, and it was Chief Attakulla-kulla himself who come upon the two lifeless bodies. He wept as he held his daughter's body in his arms and his cries were heard throughout the forest. The other searchers followed these cries and they too wept when they saw them.

The chief and his braves prayed over the bodies, and he decreed that the murdered couple would be buried in the spot where they had died. Their graves were quickly dug, and before they were lowered in, he placed a hackberry seed into the hand of his daughter and an acorn into the hand of her husband. The graves were covered, and over the years that followed, Chief Attakulla-kulla returned to the spot whenever he could and watched as the seeds he had planted sprouted into two tall and beautiful trees.

Mocking Crow never returned to the village, but he did manage to live to an old age. This, however, turned out to be less of a blessing than a curse. Just as Connestoga had predicted with his dying words, the jealous suitor never had a single moment of peace until the day he finally died. It was as though some force was dedicated to ensure that he would have no rest or comfort. He eventually lost his mind and became a hermit in the woods. He spent most of his time shouting at the voices that he heard taunting him every second of the day, and it was a measure of how strong his will to live was that it took him as long as it did to finally end his own life. He used the same knife that he had used to kill Connestoga and which Nocatula had used to kill herself.

Following his death, the land surrounding the trees that marked the murdered couple's graves was said to become a far brighter and more pleasant place to be. In 1857 a college that would eventually become known as Wesleyan was built on the land. The two trees were left alone, and word soon spread that if you visited them at twilight or sunrise, you could hear the sound of a couple whispering softly to each other above you. There were even reports of people seeing a mist surrounding the trees that almost looked liked the image of two people kissing.

Eventually nature took its toll on the trees, and they were cut down nearly 90 years after the college had been built. A marker has been erected to commemorate their existence, and to this day, people who visit the spot claim to feel a special kind of love that seemingly emanates directly from the earth.

The Mystery of the Missing Monk

The rain would not stop falling. The people of Charleston, Tennessee, prepared for the worst because they knew it was simply a matter of time before the Hiwassee River could take no more and would rise past its shores and flood the land. They took every precaution they could, but when nature decides that it's time to play rough, there is little that men can do to stop it.

When the waters rushed in, the town was spared, but the train tracks just outside of its sphere were not. The tracks were washed away in the flood before an oncoming passenger train could be alerted, and the train derailed and crashed into a nearby ravine. The sounds of the crash and the cries of the surviving wounded were heard by Charleston's citizens, who braved the waters to rescue everyone they could.

The small town had no hospital, no place to keep the wounded. People opened up their homes to these strangers and the dead were stored in a makeshift morgue inside the train depot. The town's doctor—we will call him Dr. Cooper—hurried from home to home, doing his best to care for all those who had any chance at all to survive. For days he did not sleep or rest and eventually the strain grew so great that he collapsed from exhaustion. Refusing to heed the same advice he would give, he returned to work soon thereafter and many lives were saved thanks to his efforts.

But dozens of passengers were not so lucky. These poor men and women were identified and their names were matched with the train's passenger list, and when the rain ended and the flooding ceased, there was only one passenger unaccounted for. He was a Catholic monk from Baltimore, and his body was not among those that had been collected in the small town's improvised morgue. He had not been assigned to any family to care for, and there were no remains found inside or near the train once the subsiding flood allowed for a complete and thorough search of the accident.

As far as the authorities could tell, the monk had disappeared and they had no idea where to look for him. There were many theories about where he might have gone. One was that he survived the accident unscathed, but without his memory, causing him to wander into the wilderness, where he lived liked a savage animal. Another postulated that he survived and took the accident as an omen that God did not want him to be a monk, and he walked all the way to Chattanooga and started a new life as a family man. Some suggested that he was never on the train at all, and had been murdered by one of Baltimore's many infamous gangs because he had been in possession of a piece of art owned by the church that was coveted by collectors all over the world. But the most popular of all the theories was that someone had stolen his body for reasons no sane mind could possibly understand.

Years passed and the mystery of the monk's disappearance remained unsolved, until a series of incidents at Dr. Cooper's office suggested that he knew far more about what had happened to the young man than he had ever previously indicated.

The first public incident occurred when a young boy was sent by his parents to fetch the doctor when his younger sister had suddenly taken ill. He first stopped at Dr. Cooper's house, but no one was there, so he ran to the doctor's office, hoping that the old man was working late. When he got to the building, he found that the front door was open, so he stepped inside. In front of him he saw a man dressed in a plain brown robe, with a hood over his head, obscuring his eyes.

The boy spoke to the man. "Uh, excuse me, but is Dr. Cooper here?"

The man in the robe did not speak to the boy; he instead turned away and vanished completely from sight. The boy screamed as loud as his lungs allowed, which alerted Dr. Cooper, who was reading in his office. He ran to the boy and asked him what was wrong. When the boy told him what he had seen, Dr. Cooper turned white and told the boy not to say anything to anyone about this strange incident. But the boy did not listen to the doctor and told everyone he knew about the strange man in the robe who had vanished right before his eyes. Over the months that followed, other people verified his claim when they too caught sight of this hooded phantom.

Dr. Cooper refused to discuss the matter with anyone, but, eventually, the controversy grew too great and the authorities were sent to investigate this odd paranormal occurrence. Faced with their questions, the old doctor could no longer keep quiet and he finally explained who the phantom was and in so doing solved the mystery of the

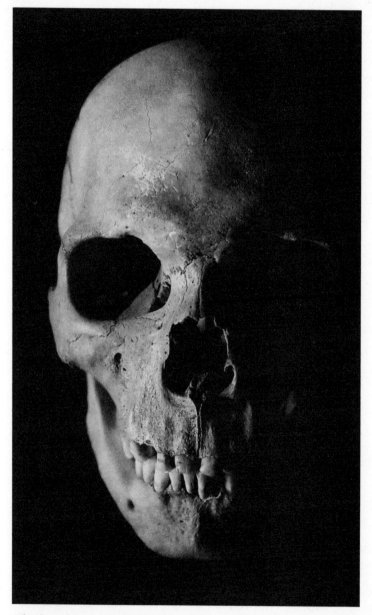

The doctor's voice trembled as he told the authorities his strange tale.

missing monk. The doctor's voice trembled with a mixture of relief and guilt as he told the authorities his strange tale.

"It all began in '67, just before the flood," he explained. "I had just moved to Charleston and several pieces of my equipment were lost during the transportation process. Most of the pieces were easy to replace, but the one that meant the most to me wasn't. It was a genuine human skeleton given to me by my father when he retired from his practice. As you can imagine, those are quite rare to come by. Most go only to universities, hospitals and other important medical establishments, and are seldom, if ever, sold to individual doctors. Those few that were available for purchase were so expensive that I could not afford to buy them. My only choice was to buy a set made of plaster, which disappointed me greatly because I had hoped to be able to give my son—if and when I had a son—a genuine specimen like my father had given me.

"I was about to order the plaster set when the flood caused the train to derail and I spent those long, horrible days taking care of all those poor wounded people. Those whose injuries were so severe they stood no chance of survival were sent to the morgue we established in the train depot. After taking care of the treatable, I went to the depot to see if there was anyone who had managed to survive the night. There was just one, a young man from Baltimore. I tried my best to ease his pain, and I talked to him for the few minutes that remained before he finally passed on. He had told me that he had joined the church because he was an orphan and that he had no family outside of his order.

"It was when he told me this that I came up with my wicked plan. Knowing that his body would never be missed by anyone, outside of a few monks who I assumed were above that sort of thing, I hatched a plan to abduct his corpse so I could obtain a replacement for my lost skeleton. I told the men who were watching over the bodies that they needed to help move some of the wounded to new homes. When they were gone, I went to my house and got out a wheelbarrow I had borrowed from my neighbor a few weeks earlier. I returned to the morgue, placed the monk's body into the wheelbarrow and returned as fast as I could to my house. I placed him in my guest room and then returned to look after more of the wounded.

"A few days later I collapsed from exhaustion and I was taken back to my house. I was horrified when I awoke because I was convinced that the people who were caring for me would smell the body decomposing in my guestroom. But luckily at that point, everyone in town was inured to the smell of death, there having been so much of it in the past few days. But not wanting to tempt fate, I got out of bed as soon as I could—far sooner than I should have—and returned to work so no one would remain in my house to discover what lay inside of it.

"Finally, after a degree of tranquility returned to the town, I took the body of the monk and transported it during the middle of the night over to my office, which had a concrete basement in which I could properly prepare my specimen. First, I had to strip the man's flesh from his bones. This was a most unpleasant task, as he was quite rotten at that point, but it had to be done. Then I boiled his bones in a large vat of water, bleaching them until they were as white as the specimens I had lost during my move. Then I had to reassemble them, using chicken wire and glue, and—at last—I had a skeleton I could someday give to my son—except the joke was on me, since I never married and never had a son to pass it on to. I had hoped that no one would notice that the man's body was missing, but someone did and everyone started talking about what had happened to the monk who had been on that train.

"I kept the skeleton in my office. I still do. It's the one in the corner right there. Doesn't it look good? Such a shame…

"Not long after, I started having these strange nightmares in which a man in a monk's robe would stand over me with a knife. I always knew what he was going to do with it— strip me of my flesh so he could boil my bones—but I always awoke before that happened. Then I started seeing him here in this building. It was always at night, when I was alone, and I thought I was imagining him. The guilt over what I had done was causing me to see things that were not there. When that boy came in looking for me and saw the monk standing there in my waiting room, I finally knew that he was not an illusion, but a true spirit intent on someday exacting his revenge.

For so many years, I tried to keep it a secret, but the boy told everyone and here you are now and I feel so relieved. It feels so good to have this burden lifted from my soul. I have carried this secret with me for so long and I do not think I could stand the weight of it a second longer."

Dr. Cooper was not charged for what he had done. Instead, he retired and his practice was taken over by another doctor. His replacement attempted to return the bones to the order the monk had belonged, but he discovered that it had been disbanded just a year after the train accident. The monk's bones were buried in an unmarked grave in a local cemetery, but this did not appear to satisfy the man's spirit, which continued to be seen at the building where his bones had been on display for so long.

In 1932, the building was torn down, and to the shock of those workers involved in its demolition, a robe and a string of rosary beads were discovered hidden inside one of its walls. The building's destruction did not keep the ghost of the hooded monk from returning to that spot. Sightings of him continue to this day, and no one knows what it will take for the spirit to finally decide that it has earned the rest, which was denied so many years ago when the rain would not stop and the waters of the Hiwassee River rose far beyond its shores.

Fiddlers Rock

When it gets cold in Johnson County, a sound can be heard from a place known as Fiddlers Rock near the top of Stone Mountain. Most people assume it is simply a trick of the wind. They are wrong. The wind has no cause to be mischievous in this solemn spot, and it has no reason to whistle out a sad song of hopelessness and despair, but there is another force at the top of the mountain that does. It is a spirit—one whose gloomy tune was once so joyful it could work miracles, but is now in such pain that most people cannot stand to listen to its dark, suicidal refrain.

It is not the wind, but the music of Old Martin, the greatest fiddle player to ever live and die in Tennessee. And the song he plays is not a random tune, but an elegy to the betrayal that would forever link his spirit to Fiddlers Rock. He plays not to forget what was done to him, but to remind all those who hear that they should be wary when approached by beautiful strangers, especially those with kind words on their lips.

No one who knew him could think of a time when the famous fiddler wasn't known as Old Martin; he was already an old man by the time fortune left him to live in Johnson County. His face was so defined by its wrinkles and creases that it was impossible to look into it and imagine what a Young Martin might have looked like decades ago. He often told people that he was born this way and that even when he was a child he looked like an old man. More than a few people were willing to believe him. Still, as long as he had his beloved instrument in his hands, it did not matter what he looked like.

There was no one in the world who could make a violin sing like he did, and sing was the right word, for when he played, the sound was closer to what one would expect from a human voice rather than a device made out of wood and metal. The sound was so beautiful it stopped babies from crying, made the sick and injured forget all about their pain and even reduced the most coldhearted scoundrel to an avalanche of tears. But his gift inspired as much jealousy as it did admiration. Other musicians who heard him play often became bitter, knowing that they would never be able to create melodies so haunting and wonderful even if they tried to play every minute of the rest of their lives. Many gave up playing rather than face their own inadequacy, but at least one fellow decided that it would be better if Old Martin would stop playing instead.

The fellow's name was Keane and he too played the fiddle, but no one in Johnson County much cared to hear him do it. Why listen to someone who was merely good when you could just as easily listen to the greatest? This simple truth burned a black mark deep into Keane's heart, and this mark made him vow to do everything he could to see that Old Martin's songs were silenced and never heard of again.

But this proved to be a far harder task than one might imagine, as there was seldom a moment when the old fiddler was ever alone. Every scheme Keane concocted to end his rival's reign of superiority was foiled by the fact that there would be at least a dozen witnesses to point the

There was no one who could make the violin sing like Old Martin did.

finger in his direction when it was completed. Plus it seemed as if there was some invisible force that surrounded the old man, which protected him from danger. One of Old Martin's favorite ways to spend the day was to go to Stone Mountain and sit on a ledge and play his fiddle, whose melodies would charm the mountain's rattlesnakes from out of their hiding places. With a smile on his face, he would entertain a dozen or so deadly snakes, as if they were no different than a collection of young schoolchildren.

Keane saw only one place for vulnerability in the old man. Though Old Martin was almost never alone, he seemed to be a stranger to romantic love. Women were entranced by his music, but his age and his shyness when he was without his fiddle kept them from ever approaching him. Though he never said so, it seemed obvious to Keane that Old Martin was lonely. And it was at this weakness the envious cad decided to strike.

But in order to do so, Keane needed to find a woman who could listen to Old Martin's music and still be cruel and treacherous enough to seduce him and then break his heart. He knew that no such woman existed in Johnson County and he doubted there was one in the entire state of Tennessee, which was why he decided to travel to the one place on earth where he was certain he could find such a venomous female. He went to New York City.

He took with him every dollar he had managed to save during the entire course of his life and he scoured the city's most disreputable locales. After a full week of cavorting with all of the wrong people, he eventually learned that he would find no female on this planet colder or crueler than Josie McCombe. In just her first three years in the city, the blonde beauty had already earned a reputation amongst New York's criminal underground as the most viperous grifter the town had ever seen. She thought nothing of taking a man with a family and good reputation in the community and seducing him until he had given her every last cent he had to give. Once her victims had nothing left, they inevitably resorted to acts of thievery and embezzlement to avoid losing her favor, and when their crimes were discovered and their lives were ruined, she would move on to her next victim, without a single second of hesitation or remorse.

Keane knew instantly that she was the right woman for the job, but he found that she was not an easy woman to meet. A full month went by before he even saw her in person. He found out that she was attending a party, where she hoped to lure a few potential suckers into her trap, so he got himself a job playing the fiddle in the band that had been hired for the event. When he finally saw her, he immediately understood why so many men had been willing to ruin their lives to spend time with her. She was not the most beautiful woman he had even seen, but she was easily the sexiest. She was, as his mama used to put it, "Sin on legs," and she had mighty fine legs for sin to perch on.

During a break he summoned all of the courage and approached her. The disdain she felt for him was obvious on her face before she even said a word.

"What do *you* want?" she asked him, her inflection making it sound like she was talking to a tiny worm.

"Miss McCombe, my name is Orville Keane and I have a business proposition for you," he answered.

"Well, *Orville*, it better be good, because you're interfering with my business right now."

For a blonde woman who barely stood five feet tall in heels, she was unbelievably intimidating. Keane wiped some sweat from his brow and he explained to her what he wanted her to do.

"How much?" she asked him when he finished.

He told her and she laughed like it was the funniest joke she had ever heard.

"Are you kidding? I don't get out of bed for twice that much."

Keane felt his only chance to get rid of Old Martin was slipping away from him, so out of desperation he decided to start grifting the grifter.

"You didn't let me continue," he improvised. "That's just how much I'll pay you to come down to Tennessee. You'll get the real money out of Old Martin himself."

This managed to catch her interest. The disdain temporarily faded from her face. "Go on…" she said.

"He's one of the wealthiest men in the state. Made all of his money from playing concerts around the world, before he decided to live out the rest of his days in Johnson County. But no one knows it, because he lives like a pauper. He has enough cash stocked away to buy the entire county if he wanted to, but you would never know it to look at him. So, like I said, I'll pay you to come to Tennessee, and when you get there you can help yourself to every last cent you can squeeze out of the old codger."

"How do you know he's so loaded, if it's such a secret?"

"I know one of the ladies who works out our local bank. She told me that it would have been out of business years ago if it weren't for his account."

"How much do you think we're talking about here?"

Keane named an astronomically high figure.

"And you say he's old and lonely?"

"They don't come much older and lonelier," he said, with one brow raised.

"How soon can we leave?"

"Tomorrow, if you like," he said.

"Good. Saves me having to spend another second at this excruciating party," she said nonchalantly.

* * *

Keane had never sat in a private car in a train before, but it was the only way Josie was willing to travel to Tennessee.

"So what's the plan?" he asked her somewhere along the way through West Virginia.

"Who needs a plan?" she replied. "If this guy is as lonely as you say he is, then all I'll have to do is smile at him once or twice and he'll hand over everything he has to me."

"I'm just worried about what will happen when you hear him play. His music can do things to people."

"It won't do anything to me. I've never liked music. Never saw the point of it. You can't spend it, eat it, drink it or wear it, so it's completely useless as far as I'm concerned," she said.

Although her words offended him deeply as a musician, Keane took comfort in the knowledge that his money had not been ill spent. If any soul could withstand the grace offered up by Old Martin's melodies, it was the jet black one that resided somewhere in Josie McCombe.

To say that she was unimpressed when they finally reached Johnson County was something of an understatement.

"This guy better be richer then the King of England if I'm going to have to stay in a dirt hole like this."

Keane assured her that Old Martin was just that rich and maybe even a little more. He didn't really worry about the fact that he was lying to her because he figured that Old Martin's heart would be crushed by that time that she found out, and it wasn't like he was cheating someone who didn't have it coming.

He found her a room in the nicest hotel room in the county, which still managed to fall far below her standards. Standing in its lobby, she stood out like a flashing beacon in a darkened coal mine. People stared at her like she was some exotic import from a far-off land, and she paid them no attention at all.

She was there for two days before Keane was able to introduce her to their target. Old Martin had been asked to play his fiddle at a local dance, and he had happily obliged.

Old Martin greeted his fellow fiddle player before the dance had started. "Hello there, Keane. You've been away for quite some time."

"I had some family business I needed to look after. My niece found herself in a spot of trouble and I needed to go to New York City to sort it out. Luckily, it's all behind us now and she came here to live with me. You should meet her." He turned and called over to Josie, who had been standing in another corner of the room.

The old man's eyes widened as he took in the spectacular sight of Josie walking toward them.

"What is it, Uncle Orville?" she asked Keane, her voice as innocent as a newborn colt.

"I want you to meet a friend of mine. This is Old Martin, the greatest fiddle player you're ever going to hear. Martin, this is my niece, Josie."

"My uncle says such nice things about you," she said and smiled.

It took the old man a moment to realize that the gorgeous young woman was actually talking to him.

"It's a right pleasure to meet you too, Josie," he said after a few awkward seconds.

"I think they want you to start, old timer," Keane told him, barely able to hide his delight.

Looking slightly befuddled, Martin turned away and headed back to the stage.

"That was perfect! He's known you for two seconds and he's already in love with you," Keane said elated.

"Almost, but not quite yet. We'll have to wait until intermission until he's mine for life," she said and grinned.

They watched as the old man walked onto the stage and put his fiddle to his chin and started to play.

Keane smiled as the dance began. He smiled because he knew that soon the music—as wonderful and perfect as it was—would be coming to an end. His smile faded, though, when he looked over at Josie and saw the look on her face.

It was a look of awe and utter astonishment.

She spoke to him without taking her eyes off of the old fiddler. "You said he was good, but I never expected anything like...*this*."

Keane was worried. "Josie, are you going to be able to do this?"

She turned her head to look at him and her face changed, as if she were coming out of a daze. "Sorry," she apologized, "I don't know what came over me." She looked back at Old Martin and reassured Keane. "Don't worry about it. I won't let this noise distract me."

* * *

Old Martin was drinking a cup of punch during the break when Josie walked over to him and stroked his hand.

"That was incredible. My uncle said you were the best, but I never expected you to be that amazing."

"Thank you," he said and blushed.

"No, thank *you*," she purred.

She let go of Old Martin's hand and walked back to Keane. "He's mine. Let's go before he starts playing that thing again."

* * *

Over the next week Josie managed to "run into" Old Martin on three separate occasions. Each time she lingered in his presence a little longer than the last, casting her spell on the lonely old timer. With each meeting she grew bolder and more flirtatious, building up his confidence to the point that he could believe that such an attractive young woman might actually find him worthy of her attention. Old Martin blushed when he saw her radiant smile.

At the end of their third meeting, he asked her if she wanted to go to another local dance where he was providing the entertainment. Keane's enthusiasm toward this development turned sour when Josie told him he wouldn't be coming to this event.

"Why can't I be there?" he asked.

"Because this is where I have to take this to the next step, and he won't be comfortable if my Uncle Orville is standing right there beside me."

"Just be careful. That music of his almost got to you before," Keane said.

"Don't worry about me. I'm a professional. I'm not going to let his sorry little tunes keep me from my earning my paycheck."

* * *

All eyes were on Old Martin as he stepped into the hall with the beautiful, young woman by his side. People whispered and stared as they struggled to comprehend what such an attractive lady would see in the homely old man. No one believed for a moment that it was because of how he played the fiddle.

The old man was too spellbound by his companion to notice the reaction their union was causing, and Josie was pretending that she too was completely oblivious to the attention they were receiving.

"You're looking lovely tonight," he said softly as they wandered over to a quiet corner.

"Thank you, and may I say that you are looking especially handsome as well."

"I don't know about that," he said. Almost everything she did and said managed to redden his cheeks.

"Are you going to play me a special song tonight?"

"If you'd like one, I will."

Josie looked over his shoulder and saw that someone was waving in their direction. "I think they want you to start now," she told him. "Will you remember to wink at me when you play your special song? It will be our little secret."

"I will," he said. "I promise."

Before he could turn around and leave, Josie gently grabbed him and gave the old man a kiss on the lips. "That's so you don't forget," she whispered.

He staggered a bit as he walked to the stage. He had not been kissed like that—or at all—in a very long time. His expression was still a bit dazed as he stood in front of everybody onstage, but his befuddlement quickly faded as he placed his fiddle underneath his chin and started playing.

For the first half hour Josie managed to fight against the powerful charms of the old man's music, even as she pretended to watch him with rapt adoration. Then he stopped and gave the crowd a wink before he began playing the most beautiful piece of music she had ever heard.

It was not natural malice that had led Josie down her wicked road, but rather a life filled with abuse and abandonment. Never in all of her childhood had she ever been exposed to anything that suggested that there was more to living than self-preservation and the collection of expensive possessions. She had never been to a museum, been given a great book or been allowed to attend a concert or play music. She did not know that even with a soul as black and foul as hers had become, she could still be so moved by a single song that it would forever change her life.

As Old Martin played his tribute to her beauty, tears began to stream down her face. She touched her cheek as though she could not remember the last time she had ever cried.

In the four minutes it took for the old fiddler to play his special tune, Josie McCombe, the coldest, cruelest woman ever to cheat a man out of his fortune, felt something inside her she had never experienced before.

It was love.

* * *

Keane could not believe what she was telling him. "You're what?" he screamed at her.

"I'm going back to New York. I can't do this. It's not worth it."

"It was his music, wasn't it? He played you something and your heart melted for him!"

"I've got to go home. Bad things will happen if I stay," she insisted.

"But you're the queen of bad things! I chose you because you were the most coldhearted viper in all of America! You felt no remorse and took only delight in seeing good men ruined!"

"I'm not that person anymore. You should forget that she ever existed."

"But I can't forget! She was my only hope of ridding me of this curse! Do you know what it's like knowing that no matter how good you are, there will always be someone who will always be better? To know that you could practice each and every hour of each and every day and never play as well as he plays? Tell me, do you know what that is like?"

"No," she answered.

"It is the worst possible hell! Give me fire! Give me brimstone! But there is nothing the Devil could do to me that I have not yet experienced here on earth!"

"I'm sorry, but I can't help you."

"All you have to do is go to him and say you never want to see him again! Do that and it will be enough."

"I told you, I can't."

"You think you have changed, but you haven't! You are as cold now as you ever were before. You see me suffering like this in front of you and it concerns you not one bit!"

"I can't stand anymore of this," she told him. "I'm leaving."

Keane stared at her with pure hatred in his eyes, but then a strange calmness came over him, which did little to ease her anxiety. "Fine. Then I will have to do this another way," he said quietly.

He reached into his jacket and pulled out a knife.

"What are you doing?" she asked.

"If you won't go see him, then he must lose you another way."

"You wouldn't!"

"My dear woman, you have no idea what a man in hell is willing to do to get out of it," he said.

She tried to run for the door, but he was too quick. She screamed as he plunged his knife deeply into her chest.

He held it there until her screaming stopped.

* * *

Old Martin was so heartbroken by the news of Josie's death that he disappeared. A week passed without him being seen by anyone, and concern for his well-being grew until a search party was organized to look for him.

He was found on his ledge on Stone Mountain. His body was covered with two-dozen rattlesnake bites. Apparently his melancholy song displeased his reptile audience and they showed their displeasure the only way they knew how.

Keane was arrested and hanged for his crime, but before he died he heard two people talking outside of his cell.

"It turns out the old man was rich! Can you believe it? He lived like a pauper but he had a fortune in the bank!"

"It takes all kinds I guess. Still, it's a shame. He played the most beautiful music."

And that music can still be heard at Fiddlers Rock, only it is a far sadder tune than anything the old man ever played during his life. Some blame it on the wind, but the wind has never known such sorrow.

The Bell Witch

Lucy Bell was a wise woman. Though at the age of 47 she could still not read or write, she was possessed by a powerful intuition that allowed her to take care of her husband John and their eight children. She had married John, who was 20 years her senior, when she was just 12 years old, and while some might have felt robbed of their childhood after such an arrangement, Lucy had no regrets. Her greatest satisfaction came from the family she had raised and the knowledge that they were as happy as she was.

During their 35 years of marriage, she had become a master of interpreting John's many different moods, even though it seemed to everyone else that he only had one—stern seriousness. Upon observing a single raised eyebrow or infinitesimal grimace or smile from her husband, she instantly knew how he was feeling, while the rest of their family and friends saw only his regular stony expression.

One day in 1817, she saw a confusion in his eyes that no one else in the world could ever have spotted, but which was to her as clear a sight as a white pearl sitting on black velvet.

"What's wrong?" she asked him as she moved away from the kitchen stove, where she had been preparing that night's dinner.

"It's nothing," he said. "I thought I saw something in the cornfield."

"What was it?"

"I wish I could tell you, but I have no name for what it was. I have seen no creature like it before, and I have never heard tell of anything like it."

"Sit down," she urged him. "Tell me what you saw."

John listened to his wife and sat down on a chair. She poured him a glass of water, which he drained with one long swallow.

"At first I thought it was a dog," he said after emptying his cup, "but as I moved closer to it, I became less and less convinced. Its body was like that of a dog—"

"What kind?" she asked.

"No breed in particular comes to mind," he admitted. "It was a mongrel's body, large and thick, without any of the characteristics that define one type from the other. It had short dark hair, with patches of white on its back and chest. Its paws were the largest I had ever seen on such an animal, but its tail was nothing but a puff of fur."

"And its head?"

"That's the thing, Lucy. To look at the body one would know instantly that the creature was a dog, but its head confounded the senses as it simply did not belong on such an animal's neck."

"What was it?"

"It was a rabbit's head. A big jackrabbit, with ears that stood straight up and a constantly twitching nose."

"Are you sure?" she asked. "Perhaps what you saw was a new breed of dog whose face is similar to a rabbit's."

"No, Mama," a voice interrupted from behind. It was Betsy, their youngest daughter who had just turned 11. "I saw it yesterday. It really is a rabbit's head."

"Where did you see it?" asked her father.

"Just outside the house. Richard and Joel saw it too. We were playing together." Richard, who was six, and Joel, who was four, were the Bell's two youngest children.

Lucy returned her attention to her husband. "What did you do when you saw it up close?" she asked him.

"I was so caught off guard by the sight of such an animal, I reacted before I knew what I was doing. I lifted up my rifle and shot at it from only a few feet away."

"Did you kill it?" asked Betsy.

John shook his head. "I didn't even wound the creature. It sped off the field at a rate far faster than any dog could ever match." He looked up into his wife's eyes. "I don't like it, Lucy," he told her as he lifted himself out of his chair. "I think what I saw might be an ill omen. Something ill is going to happen here, but I know not what."

"Nonsense." Lucy walked over and hugged him. "Since when have you ever been a superstitious fool?" she teased. "I tell you both, it was just a new kind of dog. You'll see. In a few years, Robertson County will be full of them."

With that she shooed the two of them out of her kitchen and finished making that night's supper. The strange hybrid creature was not discussed as everyone gathered for dinner. Instead, Zadok, 14, and Dewry, 21, peppered their father with questions about his life before he met their mother, which always amused them, since they could hardly imagine a world where John and Lucy had not been together. John, Jr., who was 24, teased his sister Esther, 17, about her fiancé, Alexander Porter. Betsy sat and ate quietly, while Richard and Joel giggled and played a game to see who could eat the fastest. The only family member absent from the table was their oldest son

Jesse, 27, who was having dinner with the Gunns, his fiancée Martha's family.

It was a typical dinner for the family, no different than any other, until their reverie was broken by a hard thumping sound coming from outside the house.

"What on earth is that?" John asked as the noise of the beating quickly escalated in power and rhythm. He jumped up from the table and was quickly followed by John, Jr., Zadok and Dewry as they went outside to investigate the cause of this disturbance. They found nothing. There was no one outside the house and they found no other explanation for what they had just heard.

"Ill omens," John spoke to himself under his breath, not loud enough for his sons to hear.

The next night the family was much less animated than usual as they sat down for dinner. Their hesitancy proved warranted when the loud thumping was heard once again midway through the meal. John and his sons raced out of the house as quickly as they could, but still found no trace of anyone responsible for the noise. This continued for weeks and quickly began to frighten the entire family, save Lucy, who still clung to her belief that there had to be a rational explanation for what was happening.

But even her resolve was tested when she saw what happened next.

* * *

His inability to account for the cause of the mysterious banging noise left John unusually sour and quiet as the weeks passed by. Lucy did her best to cheer him up, but there was nothing she could say or do to arouse him from his depressive state. His dark mood had been passed onto the children, who now kept mostly to themselves. It soon became Lucy's habit to fret about how she could reverse her family's downward spiral as she lay in her bed at night.

This was what she was doing when she heard a scream from the room Richard and Joel shared. Both she and her husband reacted instantly to the young boys' cries of terror, and they jumped out of their bed and raced to the room. Both boys were in tears when their parents found them.

"What just happened?" Lucy asked a nearly hysterical Richard.

"R-r-r-r-ats," he sobbed. "They were in our beds and eating our bedposts."

"You saw them?" asked their father.

"No," Richard shook his head, "but we both heard them."

Before Lucy and John could say anything, another cry was heard in the house. This time it came from the room shared by their daughters.

"Go see what that is about," Lucy told her husband. "I'll stay here with Richard and Joel."

John nodded and left for Betsy and Esther's room. When he got there, he found both of them standing on their beds, looking terrified.

"There are rats in our beds!" Betsy explained to him tearfully. "But we can't see them!"

"What's happening?" asked Zadok, as he, Dewry and John, Jr. appeared at their father's side, having all been awoken by their siblings' commotion. Jesse was away on business.

"Rats," answered John. "Look for rats. You two," he said to Zadok and Dewry, "go help your mother. You," he pointed to John, Jr., "stay here with me."

Together the two of them searched for the rats in the girls' room, but after half an hour it became clear that no such creatures were there to be found. Just as they gave up looking, Zadok and Dewry returned to tell their father that they too had found no evidence of any rodent infestation.

Since it seemed very unlikely that anyone was going to get any sleep that night, Lucy went to the kitchen and started cooking an early breakfast.

"I'm worried, Lucy." John spoke to her as she stirred the oatmeal she was making. "There is something here that wishes to torment us, but I don't know what it is."

"You will soon," she encouraged him. "It is only a matter of time before you discover what is happening here and figure out a way to stop it. I am certain of that."

John walked over to her and hugged her from behind. "I know you are," he said as he kissed her on the cheek, "and that is why I love you more than anyone else in this world."

The family tried its best to forget the events of that night as the day continued. Neither Betsy, Esther, Richard or Joel were keen on returning to their rooms when it came time for them to go to bed, but Lucy managed to convince them that everything was going to be all right. And to keep her word, both she and John sat guard that night outside the two rooms, waiting to see if the rats returned.

Having gone so long without sleep, both of them struggled to stay awake as they sat in their chairs, and both nodded off and on during the night. Lucy was in an off-state when Joel's screams woke her from her daze. She ran to him and saw with her own eyes as his blankets whipped back and forth on his bed. She quickly lifted him into her arms, but that did not stop the blankets' motion. From behind her she heard her other young son cry out, and she turned and saw that he was being smothered by his own pillow. She grabbed at the pillow with her free hand, but found she did not have the strength to move it.

"John!" she cried out. "Help me, please!"

John appeared in the room's doorway a few seconds later and stood stunned for a second when he saw what was happening to his son. Then he ran over to boy and pulled the pillow off of his face.

The screams and the sounds of the struggle had awoken the other children, who were now gathered at the door. Lucy looked at them and burst into tears, suddenly overwhelmed.

"Esther, Betsy take your brothers to your room," John ordered his daughters, handing Richard over to Esther. Betsy took Joel from her mother and the two of them went to their room.

"You three go back to bed," he spoke to Zadok, Dewry and John, Jr. "There's nothing we can do right now and we'll be useless tomorrow without any rest."

The boys went back to their rooms.

With the children gone, John walked over to his wife and tried his best to ease her tears. "You must not do this, Lucy," he told her. "You are our rock. Without you we are lost."

"But I'm so scared," she whispered to him.

"I know you are. We all are, but you have to be strong. Stronger than the rest of us combined. Whatever this thing is, we cannot let it destroy us. And it will not as long as our heart still beats. And you, Lucy, are our heart."

Lucy stopped crying and listened to her husband's words. From that moment on she would never let the force that was tormenting them affect her in that way again. Considering what it had in store for all of them, this was a greater task than anyone could imagine.

* * *

As the weeks progressed, the force that was haunting the house visited each of the Bell children as they slept at night. Their blankets were thrashed about and their pillows were thrown to the floor, although thankfully the spirit no longer seemed interested in suffocating anyone. At their father's behest, they told no one outside the family of their troubles and they did their best to let their lives go on as normally as possible.

Esther married Alexander and moved out of the house, leaving Betsy with a room to herself. For a brief time, the strange incidents ceased, allowing for the vain hope that peace had returned to the house, but this illusion was quickly snuffed out by the sound of an old woman's voice.

It was John, Jr. who heard it first. He had just come into the house from outside when he heard what sounded like a frail, whispery hollow of a voice singing a hymn he did not recognize. By the end of the day everyone else had heard it as well. Not everyone heard the hymn, though. Betsy, Zadok and their father instead heard the sound of a woman crying.

As disturbing as this was, it did provide their first clue as to the identity of the spirit. It was, they gathered from the voice, a woman who—based on her tears and fondness for hymnals—was both distraught and extremely religious. John and Lucy did their best to try and think of someone recently deceased who fit this description and who would have an interest in tormenting the Bells. They could think of only one name.

It had to be Kate Batts.

The Bell's trouble with Batts began when John sold her one of his slaves. Unable to afford the full cost of such a purchase, Batts had worked out an arrangement with John that involved her making regular payments with interest. Not long after agreeing to the deal, she accused John of overcharging her on the interest and brought in the local authorities to investigate the matter. They ruled in favor of Batts and John was forced to forgive the eccentric old woman her debt in full. While most people would be more than satisfied by this outcome, Batts was a woman who, once crossed, knew no forgiveness. She devoted the rest of her life to seeing that John was punished for his offense, going so far as to convince the Red River Baptist Church to excommunicate him. After that did not satisfy her, she publicly placed a curse on his name just a month before she died.

It all suddenly began to make sense. Of all the people they had ever known, only Batts was crazy and vengeful enough to go to such extraordinary lengths to continue tormenting John for his crime against her. But this knowledge only made things worse for them, since if the spirit really was that of Kate Batts, then they had no hope of ever being able to reason with it. In life, Batts had been a woman who could never be persuaded to change her mind, and it seemed highly unlikely that her death would have helped lift her out of the depths of her infamous stubbornness.

And if the spirit really did belong to Batts, then there would be no predicting what it would do next. As infamous as she had been for her inflexibility, she had been equally well known for her sudden mood swings and her irrational reactions to the most innocent kinds of behavior. She had been, to put it bluntly, a very crazy old woman, which meant they were being haunted by a very crazy old ghost.

Their concerns were quickly justified.

A month after the spirit's voice made itself heard inside the house, it started attacking Betsy. The angry spirit tortured the girl by pulling her hair and slapping her so hard that people could see the red marks on her face. Both Lucy and John despaired, watching helplessly as the vengeful ghost routinely beat their youngest daughter. There was no logic at all to the spirit's focus on the 11-year-old girl, as she had never done anything to earn Batts' ire when the old woman was alive.

But there was nothing they could do. The stress had such a horrible effect on John that he developed a nervous twitch the local doctor could not explain. Jesse escaped from the house, like Esther, by marrying Martha that autumn. Lucy urged her husband to break the family's silence and tell others of what was happening to them, but John was still wary of taking such an action. The community had little to do with him following his excommunication from the church, and he feared that news of his being haunted by a supernatural force would only serve to have the family shunned completely. But as the attacks on poor Betsy continued, he admitted he had no choice but to let the world know what was happening to his family.

* * *

James Johnston was the first person John told. James and his family lived next door to the Bells, and though he was a devout Christian who—despite his illiteracy—could quote whole pages of the Bible, he had never let John's excommunication get in the way of their friendship. If anyone would believe what John had to say, it would be James.

And yet, James was still unconvinced when he had heard it all the way through. "It's a prank," he told John. "Those kids of yours are having fun with you is all."

John insisted that his children had nothing to do with what was happening in their home.

"Then it's someone else. Some local kids."

John shook his head. "James, there is no way a living person could do the things I have seen with my very own eyes."

"I want to believe you, John, I do, but it sounds too wild a tale to be true."

"Then come and witness it with your own eyes!" said John. "It will take just one night and I assure you that all your doubts will be gone by the time the sun rises."

"Okay, John," James said. "If that is what it will take to believe you, I am willing to give you a night."

That evening James and his wife Jane arrived at the Bells' home, where they were treated to a fine meal prepared by Lucy. James kept his eyes and ears open for anything unusual in the house, but by bedtime he had seen nothing that convinced him that John's wild tale was true.

"I think John has lost touch with his senses," James confessed to his wife as they lay together in the Bells' guest bedroom.

"If he has, then it is contagious," she told him, "because Lucy and the children all seem to be as convinced as he is."

"They say that madness can be contagious," James said with a yawn, "but I never thought it would infect a family like the Bells."

With that the two of them settle down to sleep for the night.

Their slumber lasted for less than an hour.

James and Jane were both awakened by the sensation of their blankets whipping over their bodies. They both leapt out of the bed and watched as the blankets continued to move of their own accord. James waved his arms over the blankets and searched for any wires or strings that could be connected to them to make them move in this manner, but there were none to be found.

Then they heard the sound of a frail old woman singing a hymn neither of them had heard in years.

"In the name of the Lord," James shouted out, "who and what are you, and what do you want?"

At once the singing stopped and the blankets became still on the bed. James waited for the spirit to answer him, but it remained silent.

Shocked by what he had just encountered, he ran to John and Lucy's bedroom and woke them to tell them what had just happened. Both of them looked incredibly relieved to see that they were now not alone in their belief that their home was haunted.

James, Jane, Lucy and John discussed what they thought the spirit was and why it was there. James wasn't convinced that it was the spirit of Kate Batts. He thought the spirit's feminine voice was just a ruse employed to disguise the ghost's true nature.

"It's an evil spirit, a demon, just like in the Bible!" he theorized. "It means to torture and corrupt you until you have all been damned!"

* * *

Not long after the Johnstons' visit, the spirit's voice grew louder and bolder. No longer content to simply weep and sing hymns, it now began to speak directly to everyone. The Bells, encouraged by what happened with their neighbors, began to invite more people into their home to experience the spirit for themselves. Over and over again people asked the spirit to identify itself, but it stayed quiet on the subject until finally it was asked by a man that it appeared to respect more than the others.

The man was the Reverend James Gunn, brother of Jesse Bell's father-in-law, Reverend Thomas Gunn. He finally received an answer when he spoke aloud and asked the spirit, "Who are you and what do you want?"

"I am nothing but old Kate Batts' witch, here to torment Ol' Jack Bell to his death," came the spirit's reply.

At last the identity and intentions of the spirit were confirmed. It was Kate Batts as they had long suspected and it planned on tormenting them until John—who Batts had always referred to as Jack, when she was alive—was dead.

This news exacerbated John's nervous twitch and horrified Lucy, who was not subject to the wrath the spirit reserved for her husband. Kate's "witch" only had good things to say to Lucy and never did anything to make her suffer like John or Betsy, who both received the brunt of its abuse. The spirit only hurt her by ignoring her pleas to leave their house and spare her loved ones any more misery. No matter how much she begged it, the spirit remained as obstinate as Kate Batts had been during her life.

While everyone could understand why the spirit hated John as much as it did, no one could figure out why it was so cruel to Betsy. When asked, the spirit gave no response.

Lucy wasn't the only member of the Bell household to eventually be spared from the spirit's abuse. John, Jr. earned the "witch's" respect by constantly challenging it and insisting that he was not afraid of what it could do to him. Jesse's wife Martha was actually given a gift by the spirit, which came with an odd demand. A pair of black stockings appeared one night in their bedroom, and they heard the spirit's voice tell them that it wanted Martha to be buried in them (there is no record of whether or not she honored this bizarre request). This kind of irrational behavior only made everyone more certain than ever that the spirit wasn't lying when it said it belonged to Kate Batts.

By 1819, the Bell house had been haunted by the spirit for two years and had grown famous around the state as a result. And it was because of this fame that "The Bell Witch"—as Kate's spirit had become known—would be visited by Tennessee's first great political figure, a man who would someday be president of the United States.

* * *

Both Jesse and John, Jr. had served under Andrew Jackson during the War of 1812, when they fought in the famous Battle of New Orleans. Jackson remembered the two Bell brothers and when he heard of the "witch" that had possessed their family's home, he decided that he wanted to experience the phenomenon for himself. Jackson journeyed by wagon from Nashville with a group of other men, and before they even reached the Bell's home, they felt the power of its famous phantom.

They were about mile away from the Bell house when the wagon suddenly stopped in the road. The horses tried in vain to pull the wagon, but it would not move, despite not being visibly hampered in any way. After a long, fruitless effort by Jackson and his men to move the wagon by hand, the future president told the others that this surely had to be the work of "The Bell Witch." His words had barely left his mouth when they were answered by an invisible female voice that echoed around them.

"You may continue, gentlemen," the voice told them. "And I promise to visit you sometime after you have reached your destination."

With that the wagon was suddenly able to move again and Jackson and his men made their way to the Bell house. John and Lucy greeted the group warmly when they arrived, and Jesse and John, Jr. were both excited to be reunited with their former commander. Everyone gathered together in the house's main room and John and Jackson passed the time by talking about politics. Jackson's companions were growing weary of the two men's conversation and were beginning to wonder if the "witch" was ever going to make good on her promise to visit them again.

After a few hours, a member of Jackson's entourage informed everyone present that he was a trained "witch tamer" and that he had joined Jackson on this journey with the sole intention of ridding the house of its infamous spirit. He told everyone that he was going to force to spirit to appear before them, and when he did he was going to kill it with the pistol he pulled out of his jacket pocket.

It became immediately apparent that the spirit did not think much of the man's threat, since only a few seconds passed before the man started screaming in agony. His body contorted in front of everyone's eyes. His pistol fell to the ground and he told the room that it felt as though his body was being stabbed with thousands of pins. Still screaming, he ran out of the door and was never seen again. As soon as he was gone, the "witch" spoke to everyone, telling them that it had just exposed one of two imposters among Jackson's companions, and that the second man would be identified that following night.

Jackson's men didn't like the sound of this and tried to convince their leader to leave for Nashville that night, but he refused, insisting that he wanted to find out who among them was the second imposter. They set up camp outside the Bell house, but by the following afternoon Jackson had changed his mind. He would later confess that he would have rather fought the entire British army than face "The Bell Witch" one more time.

* * *

In 1820, Betsy—who still suffered greatly at the hands of the "witch"—was 14 when she began a relationship with a 20-year-old man named Joshua Gardner. They soon became engaged, which proved to be a decision that only exacerbated the spirit's wrath towards the Bells' youngest daughter. The spirit insisted to Betsy that she break off her engagement to Gardner, warning her that there would be horrible consequences if she allowed the relationship to continue.

The spirit's concern over this matter was extremely odd given how abusive it had been toward the young girl over the past three years. It definitely didn't help that the spirit tried to force Betsy to break up with Gardner by being even more violent with her than it had been in the past. But after having taken so many beatings from the "witch" after all those years, Betsy had grown somewhat immune to them and she stubbornly insisted that she would marry Gardner. In the end it would take the death of her father to change her mind.

By that year, Bell's nervous tick had progressed into a crippling disorder that had forced him into his bed. The "witch" continued to torment him as he lay in what would become his deathbed. It slapped at his face whenever he was overcome by one of the many seizures that plagued the last year of his life, and it often threw off his shoes from his feet.

"I'm not going to let you go easy, Ol' Jack Bell," the spirit would taunt him. "You're going to have truly suffered by the time I let your old carcass die."

It was December 20, 1820 when the spirit finally made good on its threat. Lucy had gone into their room with John's supper when she found him lying completely still in her bed. The tray clattered to the ground as she dropped it to the floor and ran to the bed. From around her she heard the sound of the "witch" laughing with delight. John was dead.

Shaken to her core, Lucy sat on the bed and began to weep. As she cried, her eyes drifted to her husband's nightstand. There she saw a small vial she had never seen before. She picked it up and saw that it contained some sort of liquid. She uncorked the vial and sniffed at it, but could not identify the liquid. Feeling weak, she stood up, walked out of the room they had shared all those years and informed her children that their father had passed on. She handed the vial to John, Jr. who examined and was also unable to determine what it contained. As an experiment he poured a small amount of the liquid into the cat's bowl. The family's tabby wandered over to the bowl right away and started lapping at its contents. Almost immediately the animal started coughing and hacking as if it had something horrendous stuck in the middle of its throat. It did this for a full minute before the poor creature finally collapsed on the ground, dead.

"I gave Ol' Jack a big dose of that last night, and that fixed him," cackled the voice of the spirit.

Enraged, John, Jr. threw the vial into the nearby fireplace. The glass vial shattered and its contents ignited in the fire, causing a giant blue flame the shot up into the chimney. At last the "witch" had gotten its wish.

During John's funeral, the spirit laughed and cheered as if it were watching the funniest play ever enacted. It interrupted the eulogies to sing a song no one had heard before about the glories of brandy. Lucy was horrified that even after his death, the "witch" refused to show her husband the slightest bit of respect.

Though their father's death affected all of his children, Betsy felt its impact the most. Still bearing the brunt of the spirit's abuse, she decided to finally accede to the "witch's" wishes and break off her engagement with Joshua Gardner.

"But why?" he asked when she told him.

"Because it seems that she hates you almost as much as she hated my father, and look what she did to him. If I marry you, she will torture you until you are a sick, feeble mass and then she will strike you dead. I could not bear that and I would rather never see you again than see you come to that much harm."

The spirit left Betsy alone after that, and in April of 1821 it told Lucy that it was going to leave them, but that it would return in seven years. In 1828, the spirit made good on its promise and stayed in the house for three weeks, spending most of that time talking to John, Jr. During their discussions, the spirit was said to have described future events that in retrospect sound eerily like the Civil War, the Great Depression and both World Wars. When the spirit finally decided to leave once again, it told everyone that it would return to visit "Ol' Jack Bell's" closest descendent in 107 years. Whether or not Dr. Charles Bell of Nashville, the descendent in question, received this visit in 1935 has never been determined.

After her husband's death, Lucy lived a quiet life before she died in 1837 at the age of 67. She never completely recovered from what the "witch" did to her family, and always felt that the kindness the spirit showed her only made her suffering that much worse. Of the children, Zadok was the first to pass on. He died from scarlet fever at the age of 23 in 1826. Jesse died 17 years later at the age of 53. Richard, Esther and John, Jr. followed him in 1857, 1859 and 1862, respectively. Dewry, who never got over what the spirit did to his father and sister, went in 1865, and was survived only by Betsy and Joel.

After breaking up with Joshua Gardner Betsy married her former schoolteacher, Richard Powell, three years later in 1824. Together they had eight children, but only four survived into adulthood. Powell suffered a stroke in 1837, leaving him in need of constant medical attention. The family was impoverished by his illness, but Betsy never once suggested that she made a mistake choosing to marry Powell instead of Gardner. After Powell died, the first nationally published account of the "Bell Witch" phenomenon was printed in *The Saturday Evening Post* in 1849. The article, which attempted to dismiss the story as a hoax, suggested that Betsy had been the major perpetrator of the fraud, which had amounted to nothing more than a desperate cry for attention. The article so enraged her that she threatened to sue the magazine if they didn't print an immediate retraction. The *Post* chose to take her threat seriously and printed an apologetic retraction in a subsequent edition.

She died in 1888 at the age of 82. Even at that late age, she never got over the psychic wounds that had been inflicted on her by the "witch's" torments. Right until the day she died she had a phobia about sleeping in a bed alone. The only way she could comfortably rest at night was to sleep between a sturdy wall and another person. She never talked to anyone outside of her family about the spirit of crazy Kate Batts, but the horrible old witch haunted her dreams her entire adult life.

The last of the original Bells to go was young Joel, who had been too young to remember any of the events that caused his family so much misery. He died at the age of 77 in 1890. Following his death, interest in the "Bell Witch" case only grew larger over the years. Even as the original witnesses to this perplexing paranormal pageant faded from existence, speculation about the true identity of the spirit and its motives became a popular hobby for many supernatural enthusiasts. This speculation has continued to this very day. Among the countless theories that have been proposed over the years, some of the most popular are as follows:

  • that the "witch" was not just one spirit, but a group of ghosts who chose to speak with one voice
  • that James Johnston had been correct in his assumption that the spirit was a demon from hell and that this infernal creature had been sent to torment the Bells after John was excommunicated from the local church

that the spirit really was the ghost of Kate Batts and her motive was nothing more than an irrational hatred of the man who tried to swindle her out of few dollars and, finally,

• that *The Saturday Evening Post* was right—the haunting was a fraud perpetuated mostly by a young girl who wanted some attention.

After almost two centuries have passed it is clear that this mystery shall never be answered. We will never know for sure who the "Bell Witch" really was, why it did what it did or even if it really existed at all, but the truth is that with a story as fascinating as this, it really doesn't matter if a few questions are left to forever linger in our heads.

3
Tormented Spirits

The Night Crew

When she was young, Sheila used to dream that she was locked inside a department store after it had closed for the night. In those dreams, she would spend hours trying on clothes, playing with toys and eating all of the candy that she could find, knowing that no one could stop her. The day after she graduated from high school, it appeared that her dream was about to come true, but she wasn't very happy about it.

"But that's so lame!" she said when her dad informed her that he had gotten her a job as a janitor on the grave-yard shift at the Save-Lots store located in the Forest Gallery Shopping Center.

"It's a fine job and you're lucky to get it," her dad insisted. "There are plenty of folks out there who are disappointed that it didn't go to them."

"Name one!"

"I don't see what you're whining about," he told her. "You'll only have to be there until the end of the summer, before you go to college."

Sheila couldn't believe what he just said. "Only? Only this is the last summer I'll ever get to spend with my friends, and where will I be? Mopping floors and cleaning toilets in Tullahoma's lamest store!"

"There's nothing wrong with Save-Lots. I shop there all the time."

"Exactly!"

"Look," he said. "I know you're disappointed because you will miss some really cool parties where all your friends will risk their futures by getting drunk and fooling around, but you're taking this job because a) you still live in this house and b) you're going to need the money if you're going to have any fun at college."

"I hate you," she said lightheartedly.

"I know you do, Punkin.'" He smiled back at her, knowing that he had won the argument.

* * *

Three other people worked the night shift at Save-Lots. Denny, the security guard, had worked there the longest, beginning back when the store was a Mono-Mart. Freddy and Vera, the other two night cleaners, had both been there for over a year. Almost immediately Sheila had decided that there was something very odd about these three people. All of them were nice to her, but they always seemed unusually tense, as if they were in constant fear of something.

For the first couple of days she had followed Freddy and learned what she was expected to do as he made his rounds throughout the store. By her third day she was ready to work alone and found that the job wasn't quite as horrible as she had thought it would be. Her biggest concern had been that she would have to clean the restrooms, but for some strange reason both Freddy and Vera insisted that they had the seniority to take responsibility for this task. This made zero sense to her. Wouldn't most people use their seniority to force the new person to do something so potentially icky? But, since their insanity seemed to work to her benefit, she refused to question their logic.

A week went by and she slowly settled into a regular, if incredibly boring, routine. As time went on, she found her coworkers' behavior more and more peculiar, if not downright odd. Freddy and Vera not only spent hours cleaning the restrooms every night (to the point where they were the cleanest facilities to be found in the entire state), but they also spent all of their breaks in them as well. When she first noticed this strange behavior she asked Denny what the deal was. He looked at her for a long silent moment, as if he were carefully formulating the right answer inside his head. Finally, just as she was starting to get uncomfortable, he shrugged and said, "Stuff doesn't seem to happen in the restrooms."

"What stuff?" she asked him. He started staring at her with the same look as before, so she just shook her head and said, "Forget it, I don't need to know."

But she did need to know, so she started paying extra attention to Vera and Freddy whenever she got the chance. She noticed how, when they were outside of the restrooms, they seemed to almost jog through the store. No, jog was the wrong word. What they did was closer to that racewalking thing she had once seen in a TV show about really weird sports. Whatever you'd call it, they never ever sauntered or strolled as they pushed their carts through the various aisles. They never even seemed to stop moving, no matter what they were doing. They were always looking over their shoulders and turning around suddenly for no reason. Once, Sheila had tapped Vera on the shoulder to get her attention, and instead of turning around, the older woman jumped into the air and sprinted as fast as she could to the women's restroom.

* * *

Freddy and Vera insisted that they had the seniority to clean the restrooms.

"Dad, I have to quit," she said to her father the next day. "It's just too weird in that place. The people I work with are freaks."

"Honey," he said disapprovingly, "what did I teach you about being judgmental?"

"I'm not being judgmental," she said. "These are the weirdest people I've ever met. They're starting to scare me."

"You see, this is why you need this job. You've lived a very sheltered life and it's time you saw what the rest of the world is like. What do you think college is going to be like? You're going to meet a lot of people who are going to seem strange to you at first, but once you get to know them, you'll get to see how normal they really are."

"I'm not stupid, Dad." Sheila started to get angry. "I know the difference between people who are eccentric and people who are batspit crazy!"

"Watch your language, young lady!"

"I said spit, Dad, not—"

"—Sheila!"

She rolled her eyes. "Fine. But I'm quitting and that's final."

"Okay," said her dad. "But if you quit, you're grounded for the rest of the summer."

"What?!" she shouted. "I'm 17, you can't ground me like I'm some 12-year-old kid!"

"Oh, I can't? Watch me."

"I hate you!"

"I know you do, Punkin.'"

* * *

Unable to quit, Sheila decided that her only other way to get through the rest of the summer at Save-Lots was to avoid her coworkers whenever she could. Unfortunately this usually meant not being able to go to the restroom when she had to, but the occasional moment of physical discomfort proved less detrimental to her mental health than getting sucked into other people's insanity.

The problem was she had to spend a large part of her time alone in the big store, which could be a truly unnerving experience if a person stopped to think about it. The place was so quiet, especially when compared to how noisy it was during the day, but—in a weird way—there were times when it didn't seem quiet enough. Along with the usual creaks and hums that could be heard in any building late at night, there were other sounds that Sheila couldn't quite explain.

A lot of these noises could be caused by drafts of wind that had swept inside the building from the outside ventilation, but there were others that defied any kind of reasonable explanation. They were the ones that—to Sheila's ears—almost sounded like words. Three days after her argument with her father, she had been mopping the floor in the toy section when she swore she heard a voice behind her say something that sounded like "Don't tease me," only it stretched the words out so it sounded like "Doooooonnnnnnn'ttttttttt teeeeeeeeaaaaaaaassssssssse meeeeeeeeeeeee." When she turned to see who was speaking to her, she saw that no one was there. "Denny?" she called out, assuming he was playing a joke on her, but a quick search around the area proved that she was alone. What made it worse was that when she went back to her mop and bucket, she accidentally bumped into a toy fire truck on the shelf, causing its electronic alarm to go off,

The place was so quiet, especially when compared to how noisy it was during the day.

which—after the eerie voice-from-nowhere thing—nearly gave her a heart attack. She quickly turned off the toy's alarm and had to sit down on the floor for a second before she felt calm enough to get back to work.

"I hate this place so much," she muttered to herself as she mopped. "No wonder the people who work here are so frigging crazy."

Despite this strange incident, the word "haunted" never entered her imagination. Sheila was not a superstitious person and she definitely did not believe in ghosts. Her explanation for what had happened that night was much more rational. Working at the store was driving her insane. She once again tried to convince her father to allow her to quit, but he refused to back down from his previous threat, so she soldiered on, hoping that she would have at least one marble left rolling around in her head by the time the summer ended. This was somewhat ironic considering that all three of her coworkers were already convinced she was crazy.

* * *

They had came to this conclusion a week after she had started working at the store, when she still hadn't clued into why Freddy and Vera spent so much time in the restrooms.

"How can she just walk around out there like that?" Vera asked. "It's like she doesn't even know that they're there."

"I blame it on the TV shows these kids are watching today," opined Freddy. "They've got their brains scrambled up so much that they don't even realize what's right there in front of them. Or she just could be stupid."

"Or maybe she really doesn't see or hear what's going on out there," added Denny.

"That's impossible," said Vera. "That's like not seeing a firecracker when it's exploding at your feet."

"But if that was true, why is there are so many people out in the world who refuse to believe stuff like this is going on? I think that in order to see it, a person has to have their mind open to the possibility that it really exists," said Denny.

"So you think she doesn't see them because she doesn't believe in them?" asked Freddy.

"Yeah," answered Denny.

Freddy thought about this for a moment. "That's the dumbest thing I've ever heard."

"Amen," agreed Vera. "That girl hears and sees all the same stuff that we do. She's just too ignorant to know that she should be afraid."

"Well, then, why don't you go out there and relieve her of her ignorance?" asked Denny.

"Because I ain't her mother," she answered him. "And if I did, she'd go around and tell everyone she knows about the crazy woman she has to work with."

"Do you think she'd really do that?" asked Freddy.

"Wouldn't you?" said Vera.

Denny thought about this. "I don't say this often, Vera, but I guess you're right. As long as this girl doesn't seem concerned about the store's various…aum…eccentricities, there is no reason for us to enlighten her, but we have to agree that if she does start to clue in, we'll try and help her come to the proper conclusions."

Denny tried to make good on this pledge when, a few days later, Sheila asked him why Freddy and Vera spent so much time in the restrooms. He tried to tell her, without actually spelling it out, but either he was too subtle or she was too oblivious, because she obviously didn't get what he was talking about. She walked away from him without the slightest clue that her life was in danger each and every time she went in to work.

* * *

Even though Denny had worked in the store longer than anyone else—going on 12 years now—he only knew a few details about how the building had come to be haunted. It all had something to do with one of the construction workers who had been hired to build the place. Supposedly it had been a young kid, just out of high school, who had yet to grow out of the physical pitfalls of puberty. His face was covered with acne, so his coworkers had instantly dubbed him something mean and cruel like "pizzaface" or "pimplepuss" and he didn't take it well. (Denny had never been able to determine what the actual nickname had been.) Whenever the boy tried to get them to stop, they would just laugh at him and push him around. He tried to quit, but his dad—who had found him the job—told him he'd have to move out if he did. With no other option but to stay, the kid became more and more depressed as he spent day after day with his coworkers taunting him. Finally, one day he had had enough and snapped. A guy working next to him called him by his unwanted alias, and he attacked the man with the hammer. Unfortunately the man was much larger, much faster and much stronger than he was and was also holding a hammer in his hand. The man swung at him with the tool and careened it into the side of the boy's head, killing him instantly.

At least that is what Denny believed had happened thanks to the little information he had learned from others. He had no idea how much was true and how much was speculative. A couple years back he went to the library and tried to find out if the boy's death appeared in the local newspaper around the time when the store was being built, but he didn't find a single article that even remotely resembled the story he heard.

Nevertheless, all the things he didn't know were easily countered by all of the facts he knew without a doubt. The ghost was real and it haunted the store and it was very, *very* angry. Denny had never seen it himself, but he had

had plenty of contact with the spirit over the years. He had heard it speak many times and had almost been killed by the vengeful wraith when it caused a heavy fixture to fall from the ceiling right above him. Luckily for him, Freddy had been there and managed to push him out of the way before it crashed onto his head. This was the incident that convinced Freddy and Vera to spend as much time as they could possibly get away with in the restrooms.

They all knew that the ghost, for whatever reason, never appeared in any form in either of the two public facilities. Denny didn't have this luxury. The requirements of his job didn't allow him to spend that kind of time in the restroom, which meant he had to be vigilant during his entire shift. It didn't help that he was constantly forced to watch over the revolving door of newcomers that filled the third janitorial position. Almost none of the new janitors ever clued into what was happening before they quit, but never in all his years had he come across someone more stubbornly unwilling to accept the store's plain paranormal truth than the young woman working there that summer.

He couldn't believe what it took to convince her.

* * *

Sheila couldn't believe the day had finally come. Tonight was her last shift at the Save-Lots before she left for college, which—as far as she was concerned—meant it was the last time she would ever have to step inside the building for the rest of her life. To say she was thrilled was an understatement. When she got there she went right to work, hoping that consuming herself in the job would make the time pass faster than if she just slacked off.

Her three coworkers were also very relieved that this day had arrived. Now they could stop worrying about what was going to happen to her and hope that her replacement wouldn't be as clueless as she seemed to be. And just to make sure the night ended without incident, Denny decided to tail Sheila as best he could and make sure she avoided any trouble. In the end this proved to be a futile effort on his part because something was destined to happen that night, and there was nothing anyone could do to stop it.

Vera and Freddy were scrubbing the toilets, as usual, when Sheila went to work mopping the floor in the toy section. It was the same spot where she had her first encounter with the building's ghost, even if she chose not to think of it that way. She was too busy working to notice that Denny was standing several aisles over, watching her from afar.

He grew tense as he watched a black swirling shape form behind her. From it came the voice of a sad and angry soul.

"Doooooonnnnnnn'tttttttttt teeeeeeeaaaaaaassssssse meeeeeeeeeeeee," it pleaded to her, just like it had several weeks earlier.

Too distracted by her work to give the voice much notice, she said, "Fine, I won't," and continued mopping, not even bothering to turn around and see where the voice was coming from.

"Yyyyyyyyyoooooooouuuuuuuu ppppprrrrroooooo-mmiiiiiiisssssse?"

"Yeah, sure, whatever," she answered.

And to Denny's amazement this seemed to genuinely appease the spirit, which faded out of sight. Over the years he and the others had all run screaming from the ghost, when apparently all it took to get on its good side was a promise to leave it alone. Shaking his head with disbelief, he turned to walk over to the restrooms so he could tell Freddy and Vera what he had just seen, when he accidentally tripped over a shoelace that had become untied. The large man flew off his feet and slammed into the display shelf next to him. The impact of his weight caused the shelf to teeter back and forth and before he could do anything about it, it toppled to the side, hitting the shelf next to it. Like dominoes, the shelf set off a chain reaction and Denny watched with horror as the shelves around him started to fall in a row.

"Sheila!" he shouted out as the toy shelf next to her came crashing down beside her.

He winced and closed his eyes, terrified that she was going to be crushed under the weight of the shelf, but he opened them when the sound of impact he should have heard didn't happen.

Sheila's voiced wavered. "Denny, what's going on?"

Denny stared at the shelf next to Sheila. It was frozen at a 45° angle, as if an invisible force was holding it up. All of the toys should have fallen onto the floor, hitting Sheila in the process, but they remained on the shelf, defying all notions of physics and gravity.

Denny spoke calmly. "Sheila, put down the mop and walk over to me."

The young woman nodded and did as she was told. As soon as she was clear of the path of the falling shelf, it toppled to the ground with an enormous clatter.

"Denny," she said. "I think this place might be haunted."

"You know what, Sheila? I think you might be right."

* * *

Sheila never did return to the store. The next summer she got a job as a waitress, which she ended up hating just as much as she did working the night shift at the Save-Lots, but she didn't tell her father that.

Freddy and Vera spent a lot less time in the bathrooms after that summer. They followed Denny's advice and promised the store's spirit that they would never tease him, and they never had to be afraid of their workplace ever again. Denny felt a bit silly that it was Sheila, the person who failed to even notice the strange entity around her, who eventually showed him how to get along with the tortured spirit. But in the end, he decided it was better to feel silly and be safe than any other alternative.

Under the Bridge

Every town has one. That peaceful spot where a young couple can go to enjoy a quiet, romantic encounter without fear of having their intimacy cut short by a nosy parent or the local sheriff. In some towns, it's a hilltop, in others a cove. In Elizabethton it used to be under the Watauga River Bridge. The emphasis here is being on *used to be*, because these days only the most clueless out-of-towner would think it safe to cavort in a spot that still remains haunted from a violent incident that occurred over 75 years ago.

As both individuals and a couple, Tom Jackson and Wanda Smithson were considered by their friends to be—even by the conservative standards of the 1930s—hopelessly and incurably square. Tom was the type of fellow who always wore a suit jacket, even when he watched football games or played horseshoes. Wanda played the organ at her church. They both worked hard at school and never questioned their elders. When they started dating at the end of the 11th grade, everyone thought they were perfect for each other. The two of them agreed; Tom proposed to Wanda at a school dance and after she said yes, they decided to have the wedding a week after they graduated.

But appearances can be deceiving, and as nice and neat and decent as the two of them appeared, they did have a secret that—if discovered—would have blown the lid off their extremely straight-laced reputations. Out of all of the young couples that lived, laughed and loved together in Elizabethton, they were the pair most likely to be found living, laughing and—their favorite—loving under the

Watauga Bridge. Behind their crisp, cool and always proper exteriors were two of the most passionate souls ever to live in Tennessee.

They were, however, the very model of discretion and they took every precaution to ensure that their secret would not be discovered by their friends or family. It was because of the strain caused by their effort to keep their trysts strictly confidential that they had decided to get married so soon after leaving school. Once they were married, they could be as passionate as they pleased and it wouldn't be anything for anyone to talk about. But with the wedding still a full month away, they had little choice but to engage in their top-secret rendezvous for a little while longer.

Early on in their relationship they had discovered that certain days of the week were always less popular than others with couples seeking entertainment under the bridge so they usually only visited the spot on Tuesdays, Wednesdays and Sundays. Mornings would have been better for them, but their schedules seldom allowed it, so they had to settle for late at night. They always had to sneak out of their homes without alerting their parents. They had become so proficient at creeping in and out of their houses undetected that they could have probably made a good living as jewel thieves once they were married, if they were so inclined.

It was a Wednesday, just 35 days away from their wedding, when Wanda, who was laying on the ground with her head on Tom's chest, remarked that they only had a handful of these visits left before they never had to meet under the Watauga Bridge again.

"I almost think I'm going to miss it," she said.

"Me too," agreed Tom. "We'll have to make sure to get back out here every now and then."

"What time is it?" she asked as they both looked up at the full moon, which illuminated the clear sky.

"Almost three," he told her after checking his watch.

"We have to get up for school in four hours. We better get going."

"I hate it when you're right like that," he said as they got up.

They started walking up toward the bridge, which they had to cross to get back to their homes. The slow stroll down the bridge that always ended their clandestine meetings was both Tom and Wanda's favorite part of their Watauga get-togethers. Given how late it always was, they had never once come across another person along the way; once or twice someone in a car had driven past them, but that was it, so they were surprised to see someone heading toward them from the opposite end of the bridge.

"Do you see that person up ahead?" asked Tom.

Wanda nodded. "I hope it isn't anyone we know."

"It couldn't be," he told her. "Who else but us would be up this late on a Wednesday? And I don't know anyone who would come to the Watauga Bridge at this time of night all by themselves."

"Still, what if it is someone who recognizes us?"

"Don't worry about it," he said. "It's still too dark out for whoever that is to get a good look at our faces."

"If you say so," Wanda said apprehensively.

Time slowed as the pair moved closer to the person walking toward them. It appeared to be a man, but they couldn't see his face. He was big, at least a foot taller than

Tom, and his clothes were very dark. Were it not for the moonlight overhead, it would be very easy to mistake the man for the shadow of some terrifying monster. Both Wanda and Tom grew nervous as the man moved closer and closer. Wanda gripped her fiancé's arm as tightly as she could and Tom did his best to look brave.

Suddenly, the man stopped in his tracks. The frightened couple watched as the large man reached into his jacket and pulled out an object from an inside pocket. At first they could not see what it was, but then a ray of moonlight glinted off its edge.

"It's a knife!" shouted Tom. "Run, Wanda, run!"

Both he and Wanda turned and started to run, but the stranger proved far faster than his bulky figure would suggest. He caught up to Wanda and grabbed her by her shoulder then turned her around and drove his blade deeply into her chest.

She did not scream. There was no time. The knife cut into her heart and she was dead before the stranger twisted the blade out of her body. Tom, however, did have time to scream. He watched helplessly as his fiancée's body fell into the arms of her murderer, who then lifted her lifeless husk and threw it over the side of the bridge. In a fit of blind rage, Tom punched him so hard that it felt like all the bones in his hand had shattered into pieces. The pain was unimaginable and he fell to his knees and began to weep. Tom could hear the madman's evil, gutteral laugh. He looked up and for just one sliver of a moment he saw the moonlight expose the attacker's face.

Tom's mind could not comprehend what his eyes had seen. The monster's face was that of a man, but not a living man. It bore no flesh and was made up only of eyes and bone—a bleached white skull that laughed at him, taking so much twisted delight in all of his suffering.

The faceless ghoul lunged at Tom and slashed him with his knife. Tom somehow found the strength to run, but he would not have made it far were it not for the oncoming car.

In the car was a man and his two sisters, who had driven all the way from California to visit their aunt and uncle who lived in Elizabethton. Millie, the older sister, first saw Tom as he staggered in front of their headlights.

"Jerome, stop!" she ordered her brother who was behind the wheel.

Jerome saw Tom slammed on his brakes. The car didn't stop in time and Tom got knocked off his feet, but he managed to get up and jump into the backseat of the car.

"Mister, you're bleeding!" Agnes, the other sister, exclaimed.

"Drive!" shouted Tom.

Jerome started to ask. "Are you—"

"Drive! Drive!" Tom yelled.

Just as Jerome was about to put his foot to the gas pedal, Agnes began to scream when what looked like a large man in dark clothes jumped beside the car's open backdoor and started to grab at Tom. Her screams caused both Millie and Jerome to turn around and see the large man attempt to pull Tom out of the car. Jerome slammed down on the gas as hard as he could and the car took off down the bridge. The large man tried to hold on to Tom, but eventually he had to let go and they lost him as they drove into town.

As they drove Tom to the hospital, he told them what had happened. The doctor in attendance did everything he could to try and save him, but he had lost far too much blood and died within the hour. Jerome, Agnes and Millie told the authorities everything that Tom had told them, and though his wounds backed up his account of being attacked, the police refused to believe that the murderer responsible for this senseless crime had a skull for a face.

The police went back to the crime scene to look for Wanda's body. Based on what Tom had told the three siblings, they looked underneath the bridge, but it was nowhere to be found. Wanda's body was never recovered, and the mystery of her and Tom's murder was never solved.

From that day forth, Watauga Bridge's status as Elizabethton's premier make-out spot immediately ceased. People were warned to stay away from the bridge at night, and though no one has yet to meet the same fate as poor Wanda and Tom, some have reported seeing a figure in black lurking in the darkness. Those who have driven across the bridge have also claimed to hear the sound of someone trying to get inside of their vehicle or sometimes even the sensation of a presence sitting down in the back seat of their car.

Not everyone believes that this is the work of the skull-faced man in black. Others believe that its the spirits of Tom and Wanda once again attempting to get away from the site of their foul and violent murders. If this is the case, then the story is especially depressing because it suggests that these two lovers are now obsessed with getting away from the one place where they experienced so much of their happiness.

The Screamer

Visitors to the small community of White Bluff in Tennessee's Dickson County have commented to locals from time to time about the ravaged foundation of a house found deep in the valley. Each time this happens, the locals are quick to warn those travelers to stay away from that property lest they meet the same fate as the family who once lived there.

The legend goes back to just a few years after the Civil War, when a farmer who had trouble sleeping at night thanks to the sound of horrible cries coming from somewhere within the valley. Whenever he heard them, he would wake his wife and ask her if she had heard them as well. She would always tell him that she heard nothing and scold him to go back to sleep. The next morning he would always ask his son and his daughter if they had heard any odd noises come from the valley during the night, and they would always tell him that they had not heard a sound.

It didn't take long for his family to become concerned about the farmer's sanity. His wife urged him to stop working so hard, fearing that his duties were having a negative effect on his mind. He tried his best to honor her wishes, but he still kept hearing the sound of screams echoing through the night.

Eventually it became more than he could take, and he decided that the next time he heard the screams, he would head out into the valley and search for the spot where they were coming from. Two days later he was once again

It was an idyllic setting for a home—except for the horrible cries that he heard at night.

awakened by these agonizing shouts of pain and terror, and he reacted immediately. He got out of bed, got dressed and found his rifle. With his two bloodhounds, he started walking in the direction from which the screams appeared to be coming.

He walked for an hour, but he seemed to get no closer to the source of the sound. In fact, the more he walked, the further away the cries seemed to be, as if the creature responsible for them was moving away from him. His hounds seemed unable to catch any scent that would help him in his search, and he was about to give up when he heard screams coming from behind him, from the direction of his house.

Whereas the screams he had heard before had been impossible to identify—being neither from a man or an animal—these anguished cries were too obviously human.

"What have I done?" the farmer cried out as he started running back toward his home.

It was a long way to run, but not once during the entire time, did the screaming stop. Instead the screams grew louder and more horrible with each step he made toward his house. Despite his years working in the fields, his heart and lungs were not used to this kind of physical effort, and he was close to collapsing when he finally made it to his home. It was only when he opened the back door that the screaming he had heard finally stopped.

He walked inside and found nothing askew in the kitchen. He stumbled through the hallway that led to the room he shared with his wife and found that it was empty. He turned around and walked to the house's front room and saw that nothing was astray. He made his way to the room shared by his two children and opened it, once again expecting to find no one there, but his expectations were dashed when he discovered the mangled bodies of his family strewn about the room. Never in his life had he seen a sight so horrible or gruesome. Whoever was responsible for this vicious crime had shown not the slightest ounce of mercy or humanity.

The farmer fell to his knees and wept. Among the scattered gore and blood, he looked down at the floor and saw strange imprints in the wood. It appeared as though the footprints of the monster that had committed this atrocity were burned into the wood. As he stared at them, he heard the sound of screaming coming from outside his house. He ran to the nearest window and saw the figure of man-like creature covered in a haze of white mist. This creature screamed once again before running into the valley.

The farmer ran outside to the spot where the creature had stood and saw the grass underneath its feet was burnt black. Seeing this, the farmer went back into the house and wrote a note describing what he had seen and experienced that night. He explained that he was going to take his rifle and his dogs to follow the creature's scorched footprints until he found the monster and got his revenge.

The man was never seen again.

Visitors who are told this tale are not only warned to stay away from what remains of this grisly site, but also to never approach the misty figure that can still be spotted wandering through the valley. And if they hear the screams of something not quite human, it is best to pretend that they have heard nothing at all.

The Bleeding Mausoleum

One must wonder what the Grim Reaper thinks of grave-yards, crypts, mausoleums and all of the other monu-ments to his work. Does he feel honored by them or does he scoff at the sentiment inherent in their existence? These places, after all, are meant to comfort the living and—with a few notable exceptions—mean little to those who are left to forever reside within their boundaries. Or do these places tempt him? Does he, upon seeing another grand temple of mourning, feel himself compelled to work that much harder until he has ensured that its every vacancy has been filled?

Before you dismiss such a fanciful idea, consider the story of the beautiful white stone building that rests behind St. Luke's Episcopal Church in the town of Cleveland, Tennessee. In it resides a family that was all taken by the Reaper before they could be allowed the honor of a natural death. Each one was claimed by a sepa-rate accident, filling their familial mausoleum far sooner than anyone could have ever expected, and though they seem not to be angry over the Reaper's haste to see them together in death, they are far from satisfied with their fate. One of them haunts the land on which their white stone shrine rests and the others express their eternal dissatisfaction with blood.

John Henderson Craigmiles first came to Cleveland in 1850. A Georgia boy, he and his brother, Pleasant, moved to the small Tennessee town to open up a general store, but the life of a merchant proved unexciting for a man of

John's ambitions, so he decided to leave his brother and head out west to make his fortune in the California gold rush. But if the life of a merchant was simply boring, the life of a prospector was dangerous, backbreaking and full of constant disappointment and frustration. He gave up his hunt for gold, but he stayed when he concluded that there was money to be made by shipping the supplies needed by those other victims of gold fever who had yet to lose their hearts for the trade. He quickly made a fortune, which he just as quickly lost. Five of his six ships were hijacked by their mutinous crews, and his creditors' claims were edging him ever closer into bankruptcy. But with grit, determination and a loan from his brother, Green, he rebuilt his tiny shipping empire. Seven years later, John returned to Cleveland as a very prosperous man.

Back in the small town where his business life had started, he met the beautiful daughter of the local doctor. Her name was Adelia Thompson, and after a long and romantic courtship they were married in December of 1860. The years that followed the marriage were good ones. Though the country was embroiled in a war between the states, John's fortune only grew larger, and by 1864, he and Adelia were blessed by the birth of their first child, a girl they named Nina.

Few people in this world are lucky enough to be born as loved as the Craigmiles' first child. From the first moment he saw her, John believed she was the most perfect accomplishment of his extremely successful life, a feeling that was shared by his father-in-law, Dr. Gideon Thompson. Together the two men doted on the girl like she was a princess to be protected at all costs. She wanted for nothing, yet—thanks to some hard work by her mother—managed to avoid becoming as spoiled as other children who lived such privileged lives.

But fortune can favor a man for only so long before it grows fickle and decides to turn against him. For John that time came on a cold October afternoon in 1871. As Dr. Thompson had so often done before, he decided to take his granddaughter, Nina, for a ride around town in his buggy. She had always loved the trips the two of them made together, and as John watched them ride off, Nina was beaming from ear to ear with happiness.

Dr. Thompson had never before had trouble with his horses, but today they were strangely hesitant and slow to respond to any of his commands. Nina seemed not to notice, but he grew concerned by their odd behavior and decided it was time to return to the Craigmiles' home. As they rode back, he saw a train in the distance traveling along the tracks that crossed over the road ahead of them. He tried to slow his horses to a stop, but they kept on moving. He shouted at them, but his anger only made them gallop faster. To his horror, he realized they were on a collision course with the oncoming train. He dropped his reigns and tried to grab Nina, but his body was old and not ready for such swift movement. The horses reached the tracks just as the train crossed the road and the buggy exploded when the two vehicles crashed together. He, by some miracle, was thrown clear and only suffered a few minor injuries, but Nina, the Craigmiles' beloved only child, was killed in an instant.

Her death nearly destroyed John and the rest of his family. At her funeral he was barely able to stand and he could not speak. The only thing that saved him from complete spiritual annihilation was his conviction that his daughter's memory would be honored with a gesture that would affect the whole town. As a member of Cleveland's Episcopal congregation, he and his fellow followers had gone without a regular meeting place for years, so it seemed obvious to him that he would honor Nina by building her a church.

It took him three years, but when he was done, St. Luke's Episcopal Church was one of the finest cathedrals in the state. But John did not let it end there. Behind the church, he built a beautiful white marble mausoleum, into which Nina's body was placed. To watch over her, a group of stone angels perched on the edge of the building's roof. It was, John insisted, the only fitting monument he could think of for so angelic a child.

But if John thought that building the church and the mausoleum would help ease his pain, he soon learned otherwise when his and Adelia's second child, a boy, died only hours after he was born. Their grief over this second loss was such that they could not even bear to give the boy a name; instead, they simply placed him beside his sister in the marble tomb behind the church.

John and Adelia gave up having any more children after that. Time passed and though their pain lessened, it never completely went away. At the beginning of 1899, John slipped on a patch of ice while walking downtown. He thought nothing of it, but Reaper wanted him, so the injury grew infected and he was dead from blood poisoning by the end of the week. As he wished, he was laid to

Behind the church, John had a white marble mausoleum built in honor of his daughter's memory.

rest inside the mausoleum and at last reunited with his children.

For a time it appeared that Adelia would be allowed the natural death denied to the rest of her family, as she lived 29 years after the death of John. She had remarried a man named Charles Cross and lived a fairly uneventful life until September 1928 when she was struck down by an out-of-control automobile. As she wished, her body was placed inside the white marble mausoleum with her first husband and their children.

But Adelia's death does not end the Craigmiles' story. The first part of their second chapter actually began not long after Nina had been interred in the family tomb. The caretaker who had been hired to tend to the church and its grounds was passing by the mausoleum when he noticed a series of strange red splotches on one of its sides. He touched one of these splotches and felt that it was still wet. He examined the stain left on his finger and saw that it was not paint or any kind of sap but a substance that—against his better judgment—appeared to be blood. Lacking any other explanation for how this substance got there, he assumed a cat had caught a small animal in the spot and had been a little too enthusiastic in its decimation of the poor creature. He grabbed a rag and wiped the blood away, only to be shocked to see that it had returned the next day.

As the weeks passed, wiping the blood away grew more and more difficult until a permanent stain was left in the spot where it had first been seen. It was left alone after that and no one thought anything of it, until the death of the Craigmiles' second, nameless, child. When his small body was interred inside the tomb, another permanent stain formed on the side of the stone building. Another red stain appeared following the death of John, and a last one appeared after the death of Adelia. Around the town, the structure became known as the "Bleeding Mausoleum," and no rational explanation was ever offered for the bloody stains.

And along with these stains, there have been several reports over the years of children—it's always children—claiming to have seen a young girl, around the age of seven, playing outside the mausoleum, dressed in clothes that are at least a full century out of date. The ghost of young Nina has not displayed any signs of sadness, yet her spirit still remains at the spot where her body has been at rest for over 130 years, which says a lot about how much the Craigmiles' tragic story has affected the family in their afterlife. It is easy to believe that—even with as fine a resting place as any man, woman or child could want—they have yet to find anything that resembles peace.

Perhaps, then, the lesson of this tale is simple. Be it a glorious marble mausoleum or an unmarked grave, it matters little where a person's body is laid to rest if their spirit is not ready to pass on.

The Crash Site

When faced with an emergency, panicking is always the least helpful method a person can choose to deal with it. In virtually every stressful situation a person can face, a calm and rational mind is a must. Panic, and it's pretty much guaranteed that you'll fail to accomplish your nerve-racking goal, whatever it may be.

But as the case is with most truths like this, there are exceptions to the rule, and one can be found around Smith County's Dean Hill Road. It is here, at this lonely stretch of barely paved gravel, that a person can find him or herself in a situation where panicking is the only way out. Be as calm and rationale as you please, but you will not be set free until you have let your anxiety take over and you begin to lose control of your mind.

It happens only late at night to those who are driving alone down the road. From out of the corner of your eye you'll see something that shouldn't be there, but you won't be able to tell what it is. You'll stop your car and get out to investigate, but you'll find nothing. Then you'll try to restart your car so you can leave, but it won't start. No matter how many times you try or what you do under the hood, the engine will not turn and the night will grow darker as your situation becomes more and more desperate. If you have a cell phone, you'll discover that it has no reception and you'll realize that there is nothing you can do. It's impossible to know how long it will be until another car drives by, as the Dean Hill Road has never known that much traffic. With no other option, you keep trying to start the engine, growing more and more anxious with each attempt, but it is only when you lose control and truly start to panic that the engine will finally turn. As it revs, your heart will be pumping so fast that it'll feel ready to burst, and you'll pound down on the gas pedal so hard that the car will propel down the road like a man who has just seen a ghost. And in a way, it has.

This strange phenomenon started with an incident that occurred in 1952, when a private plane flying over the area fell from the skies. There were five people in the small plane: three men and a young mother with her baby. No one knows where they were going or where they were coming from. No evidence could be found in any airport log of such a plane taking off from any recognized destination, which has led some people to speculate that the plane was involved in a criminal activity. If this was the case, no evidence of illicit goods were ever found in the crash, though it has been suggested that the plane could have just dropped off its illegal cargo or been on its way to pick it up. Many refused to accept this theory, thanks mostly to the presence of the baby on the plane. It was generally believed that the plane was only out on a pleasure trip, and when problems occurred, the owner and pilot hadn't had the plane long enough to be aware of all of the proper aeronautical protocols.

Whichever is the case, the plane crashed in the valley that sits separated by the Dean Hill Road and the Billy Smith Road, an equally desolate locale. No one survived and none of the passengers were ever identified. The cause of the crash was never satisfactorily determined, the most likely theory being that the aircraft suffered engine failure and the man at the controls did not have the training or experience to properly handle an emergency landing.

The engine failure theory for the crash may shed some light on the strange stalled car phenomenon. Like so many other spirits who died in unlucky accidents, the five victims of the Dean Hill Road airplane crash are compelled to make unwary travelers feel the same panic they did when their aircraft hurtled downward.

The car trick is not the only way these spirits have made themselves known. All five of them have been spotted as misty figures, both together and individually (except for the ghost of the baby, who always appears with its young mother). In these occurrences, the people who have spotted them have been on foot and were not forced to interact with them like those who have been tormented with the stalled car trick.

After five decades, it appears that these five ghosts are not going anywhere anytime soon. By forcing others to reenact their terror, their intentions are not so much evil as they are sad and desperate—they simply long for others to empathize with them. Nameless and alone, they do what they do because it keeps their memory alive, even if it is a memory of a mystery that is yet unsolved.

A Jar in the Ground

For the faculty and students at Memphis' Brinkley Female College, February 21, 1871 started out as a normal day, but by the time it ended, the most bizarre unsolved mystery in the history of the state of Tennessee was firmly set in motion. It all started with two young girls. The first was a 13-year-old named Clara Robertson, who was a student at the college, and the second was an unnamed girl of indeterminate age, who definitely was not.

Classes had ended, and Clara was alone in the music room, practicing her scales on one of the school's pianos. She was not naturally musically inclined, and she considered this task a chore to be suffered through rather than an enjoyable detour from her studies. With an expression of pained obligation, she pounded at the keys, not even cognizant of the sounds she was producing. Her father believed that all young ladies should be able to play an instrument, so she practiced in the music room every day, and she cursed how the hour never seemed to end while she sat on a piano bench.

Thankfully, the hour was almost up. She yawned and stretched her arms and as she looked up from the keyboard, she caught a glimpse of something and screamed before she was even fully aware of what she was seeing.

There in front of her stood a girl dressed in pink. At least it seemed like it had once been pink, but much of its color had faded. It was covered in dirt and worms and it smelled like a horrible mixture of sulfur, rotting meat and moldy bread. This outfit alone would have warranted a scream from Clara, but what had truly caused her to cry out was the girl's face. It bore the traces of innocence one could expect to find on a young girl close to Clara's age, but the image was undone by the way the girl's flesh hung off her bones, loose and no longer attached. Her face looked like a mask and the rest of her flesh looked like a suit she wore underneath her dress. It appeared as though she wanted to say something important to her, but before she could let out a single word, Clara jumped off of her piano bench and ran screaming out of the room.

Other teachers and students who were similarly engaged in extracurricular activities poked their heads out of classrooms to see who was making all of this noise. As they stared, a teacher named Jackie Boone stepped into the hallway and stopped Clara in her tracks.

"Miss Robertson, what do you think you're doing? That's no way for a young lady to behave," she scolded the terrified young girl.

Clara was breathless and at a loss for words. "I saw a...a..."

"What did you see?" asked Miss Boone, as a crowd of students and other faculty members began to form around them.

"A girl," Clara answered. "But she wasn't a girl, she was a...a..."

"A what?"

"A ghost!" Clara finally blurted out.

Everyone, including the Miss Boone, burst out in a gale of laughter.

"It's true!" Clara protested. "I saw a ghost!"

Her passionate insistence only made the students and the teachers around her laugh even harder than before.

"Why won't you believe me?" she asked angrily.

Miss Boone regained her composure and silenced everyone with a gesture. "Enough. You're far too old for this nonsense, Miss Robertson. We here at Brinkley College expect far more from our students than to indulge in absurd childhood fantasies."

"But I did see a ghost!"

"That's it," said the teacher. "We'll see what your father has to say about this!"

* * *

As it turned out, Clara's father, a local lawyer named J.R. Robertson, was more amused than angered by the news of his daughter's outburst. "You'll do anything to get out of playing that piano won't you, sweetie?"

"I swear I saw a ghost, Papa. Why won't anyone believe me?"

"Because it sounds like hogwash," he said and smiled at her.

"But it isn't!"

"If you say so. Now go and wash up. It's about time for supper."

"Yes sir," she mumbled dejectedly.

That next day, the whole school was buzzing about Clara's ruckus and the rumors passed quickly through the halls like a series of unstoppable flash fires. The common consensus was that Clara was just making a fuss to get some attention, but some thought was given to the possibility that she had seen a ghost and who that spirit might have been.

"I heard that Sarah Foster saw Mr. Brinkley in the library last year," one girl whispered to her friends during a dull math class. Mr. Brinkley was the school's esteemed founder, who had been dead for several years.

"Sarah Foster is a liar," another girl whispered back. "Anyway, I heard it was a girl ghost and not some old man."

As the different theories and questions circulated around the campus, it soon became clear that Clara wasn't going to be there to answer them. Her seat was empty in all of her classes and no one had heard from her.

Clara refused to even consider the possibility of returning to the place where she had seen such a horrible sight. Her father did everything he could to persuade her to return, but she was so obstinate. He could tell that her fear was genuine and not simply an excuse for truancy. He knew he couldn't threaten her to get her to go back, so he decided to do the one thing he knew would get her to return to school.

"Clara, if you stop this nonsense and go back to school, I promise that you'll never have to play the piano ever again."

For the first time since she saw the ghost, Clara's eyes lit up. "Do you mean it?" she asked.

"I give you my word," he vowed.

Clara was back at school the next day. She paid no attention to the stares she received or the whispers she heard behind her back, and within a few days everything was back to normal. That is until the day she found herself alone in the library catching up on the work that she had missed during her absence. She was busy attempting to solve an annoyingly difficult math question when she heard the sound of a book falling off a shelf in front of her. She looked up, and this time she managed to stop herself from screaming.

It was the same girl as before—the one in the pink dress, whose sallow, gray skin sagged like a slowly leaking balloon. Though Clara had managed to keep herself from screaming, her instincts still told her to run. She was about to bolt for the exit when the girl moved closer to her and spoke.

"Wait," said the girl. "I have to talk to you."

Clara froze. She remained on her feet and glanced toward the library door, but she did not move.

"I'm not going to hurt you," the ghost continued. "I need your help."

Clara listened, but she did not respond.

"Outside of the school there is a tree stump. Do you know the one that I mean?"

Clara nodded.

"You have to go to it with a shovel and dig until you find a small glass jar buried in the ground. Can you do this?"

Clara nodded again.

"But you have to do it by yourself. You can't have any—"

Before the ghost could continue, two very different screams echoed in the library around them. Clara turned her head and saw Miss Boone standing with a student at the library door. Frightened by their screams, the ghost vanished from their sight. Miss Boone and the other student stopped screaming and just stood there, unable to fathom what they had just seen.

"I told you I saw a ghost," Clara said to Miss Boone in the silence that followed.

* * *

The first thing Clara did when she got home was go to her father. She told him what the ghost had said to her. Though he was quite skeptical about the details of her story, he decided to humor her and went out to gather some people to help him dig around the old stump in front of the school. Because of the sudden interruption that had occurred as the ghost had been giving Clara her instructions, she had forgotten the rather important caveat that she alone was supposed to dig for the jar, so she did nothing to stop him.

The sun was starting to set as her father and his friends gathered around the stump and started digging through the earth. No one worked very hard, since they all assumed they were simply easing the mind of a frightened young girl, but an hour later one of the diggers felt his shovel hit something foreign in the soil.

"I...I think I've actually found something," he told everyone. He bent done and removed the remaining dirt with his hands until he found a small brown jar.

"Oh my word," said Mr. Robertson. "You really did see that girl, didn't you, Clara?"

"I kept telling everybody, but you wouldn't believe me."

The man holding the jar grabbed its metal lid and was about to lift it off when Clara heard a familiar voice speak behind her.

"Don't!" said the voice.

Clara turned and saw the girl in pink behind her.

"There she is!" she said and pointed to the apparition.

The small glass jar was found near the old stump in front of the school.

Everyone turned her way and it became quickly apparent that some of the men saw the ghostly girl in pink while others did not.

"You were supposed to dig up the jar," the ghost said to Clara. "No one else was supposed to touch it."

"Oh, I forgot about that part. I'm sorry," said Clara.

"Since you did not find it by yourself, you have to wait 60 days before it can be opened. Any sooner than that and it will mean disaster for you and your family."

"Did you hear that?" Clara asked the men.

Her father had been a member of the group who could not see the ghost, but the man who had found it—the one who held it in his hands—was one of the fellows who could, and he handed it over to Clara.

The man repeated what he had heard to the others whose senses had not allowed them to experience the paranormal event that had just occurred. "We're going to have to wait 60 days until we find out what's in it, fellows."

The next day, word of what happened at the stump and the discovery of the jar spread all across Memphis and soon people were hearing about it all through the state and even as far away as Missouri. Thanks to the descriptions supplied by Clara, Miss Boone and all of the other eyewitnesses, the ghost was identified as belonging to a young girl named Lizzie Davis. She had been dead for over a decade by that point, but people still remembered that she had been buried in a pink dress. Before the building had been transformed into a school, it had been a mansion owned by a Colonel Davis who had sold the property to Mr. Brinkley a few months after the mysterious death of his only daughter.

Colonel Davis was now dead himself and was not available to supply any answers to the questions everyone had about the appearance of his daughter's ghost or the mystery of what was hidden in the jar. People's curiosity grew to a fever pitch and it dawned on Mr. Robertson that a profit could be made from this sudden interest in the jar that was in his possession. A shrewd man, he decided to rent the Greenlaw Opera House for the night the jar was to be opened and he advertised that people could buy tickets to witness the event for the outrageous sum of $1.00 per person. As expensive as this seemed, few people complained and the event quickly sold out.

Unfortunately, his advertising fueled even more speculation over the contents of the jar—speculation that soon reached the ears of Memphis' less savory citizens. Rumors that the jar contained valuable diamonds and jewels or even a treasure map that would lead to even greater riches passed through the town's criminal underground, and it was just a matter of time before someone decided to find out if these rumors were true.

Just three days before the jar was to be opened at the opera house, a trio of thieves decided to break into the Robertson's house. Not the most competent crew in town, they made far too much noise attempting to get in, and they awoke Mr. Robertson, who went outside to investigate. He found the three men and threatened to have them arrested, but the men ignored his threats and attacked him. They beat him until he told them where he had hidden the jar. He had lowered it with a string down through one of the seats in the family outhouse, which he then nailed shut, so no one would accidentally see it. The three thieves left him bleeding on the ground, found the jar and were never seen from again.

Thanks to the efforts of these thieves, the mystery of what was in that jar and why it was so important to the ghost of Lizzie Davis was never solved. Lizzie was never seen again, although Clara did later claim to have spoken to her during a séance, when the young spirit was said to have told her that the jar did in fact contain $2000 worth of valuable trinkets. But many people doubted that Clara ever really did have any contact with Lizzie after that night at the stump. Many were not satisfied with the conclusion that the jar merely contained some gold coins and jewelry. If that was the case, why was it so important to Lizzie that it be found? And why did she insist that Clara find it herself and then, later, that it could only be opened 60 days after it had been discovered? Sadly, these are questions that are likely to never be answered.

As for the college where all of this occurred, it was demolished 101 years later in 1972, after having been shut down by financial problems several years before. Few people walking down Fifth Street in Memphis are even aware that it was ever there or that it was the sight of one of their state's most famous paranormal occurrences. It is probably for the best, since there are few things as frustrating as knowing about a mystery whose solution will never be revealed.

The Cemetery by the Lake

Emily could not sleep. Her legs ached and not even the heavy blankets that covered her could keep her from feeling the constant chill that laid its frost deep within her fragile bones. She heard a sound from outside of her room and she looked up from her pillow to see a dim light shine through the crack between the floor and the doorway.

"Roger? Is that you?" she asked weakly.

"Yes, my dear," he answered as he opened the door. The light she had seen came from the oil lamp he held in his right hand.

"I can't sleep," she complained. "I try to close my eyes, but my legs hurt so much and I feel so cold."

"I thought as much," he answered. "What you need is a bit of exercise to warm you up and properly tire you out."

"Exercise? But the doctor—"

"I know what the good doctor said, and I've no intention on having you walk by yourself. This afternoon I went out and purchased a wheelchair so you can at last get out of this infernal bed. I thought now would be a good time to try it out. We can go and visit the lake."

"But it's so late."

"And why should that worry us? I have a lamp, the night is clear and the moon shines bright. The night sky is so amenable to us this evening; it might as well be day. Come, it will do you a world of good."

"It would be nice to get out of this bed…" she said.

"Don't be afraid," he said to her kindly. "I'll be there with you and if it proves to be too much for you to take, we'll come right back here."

She thought of how long she had spent in her bed, staring at the same yellow wallpaper for weeks on end. There were days when she thought she was about to go mad and start chewing on the furniture, were it not for the constant attention of her beloved husband. She knew that Roger only had her best interests at heart, so if he thought she would benefit from a nighttime excursion to the lake just outside their home, then it was silly for her to question him.

"That sounds good," she answered him.

Slowly and carefully, he helped her get dressed in some warmer clothes and then lifted her out of her bed and carried her downstairs to where her new wheelchair was waiting for her in their immaculate white foyer.

"How have you managed to keep this so clean?" she asked, not having traveled downstairs in several months. "What with work and taking care of me, I don't see how you could have the time."

"I hired someone to come in and do some cleaning for us a couple of weeks ago," he said as he sat her down into the chair.

"You did? You never told me."

"Really? I'm sure I mentioned it. Maybe you weren't in a state to pay attention to me when I did," he said while he tucked in a heavy blanket around her body.

She admitted that it was possible she had forgotten. "Who is this person?"

"Her name is Rosie. She comes in three times a week to tidy up the main part of the house."

"Why not upstairs as well?"

"Because I did not want her disturbing you."

"I wouldn't have minded the company," Emily said.

"You do not need company, you need rest."

"I know," she agreed sullenly. "This blanket is very heavy."

"I bought it from the same company that sold me the wheelchair. If it doesn't keep that chill out of your bones, nothing will. Now are you ready?"

"Yes, I think so."

"Then let us get outside and breathe in some of that fresh, rejuvenating air."

Roger opened the front door and Emily's face was immediately hit by the pleasing sensation of a cool, gentle breeze.

"That feels wonderful already," she said and sighed happily.

"I thought you'd like it." Roger smiled as he pushed her and her new chair out through the doorway.

Emily closed her eyes and marveled at how clear and new the air around her smelled and felt and tasted. She couldn't remember how long it had been since she had been exposed to anything that felt as comforting as this. There was only one window in the room and it had been nailed shut years ago. Roger had asked the doctor if it would be all right to open it, but the old physician had advised him not to, fearing what a cool breeze might do to Emily if she was alone and unable to get to the window to close it.

Roger started pushing her down the path that led from their house to the small lake that had so entranced them when they moved to the area seven years earlier. Before

During happier times, Roger and Emily used to paddle the small rowboat to the cemetery.

she had become ill, the two of them used to enjoy rowing their small boat to the other side of the water and wandering through the old Greenwood Cemetery, where they would stop and look at the graves of all the couples who had been buried beside each other. Emily had always thought that it was the most romantic thing in the world, to be with your partner for eternity. It seemed so fitting and perfect and true.

It only took a few minutes to get to the lake, and when they did tears started welling up in Emily's eyes. "It's so beautiful," she whispered as those tears fell down her face. And it was. The moon was full and they could see it reflected in its full luminosity in the water's calm surface.

"I'm so glad you took me out here. I needed this more than you could ever know."

"I thought you might like it," he answered, but his voice was not able to contain his obvious sorrow.

"Roger? What's the matter?" She turned in her chair and saw that he too was crying.

"I didn't think it would be like this," he said. "She said it would be so easy."

"What are you talking about? Who said what?"

Roger covered his face and began to cry. "You don't know," he said as he wept. "You don't know how hard this has been for me."

"But I do, my darling. I do know, but we'll get through this, and when we do, we'll both be healthy and happy again."

He shook his head sadly. "I can't...I can't wait that long. I just don't have it in me."

"Roger, I don't know what you're saying, but you're beginning to frighten me."

"She said it would be easy," Roger said quietly.

"Who said that, Roger? What would be easy?"

"All I would have to do is push you in, and say it was an accident."

"Roger! What are you saying?"

"Tell them that I went back to the house to fetch you another blanket and that you were gone when I came back. I went in to the water to save you, but it was too late, you had already drowned."

"Roger! Stop it! You've gone mad."

"She said it would be easy."

"Roger, get a hold of yourself. Think about what you are saying!"

"I can't…It's been so hard."

"Roger!"

Emily could do nothing but sit and watch as her husband began pushing her wheelchair toward the calm, cool water. She pleaded with him to stop, but it was clear that he would no longer hear anything that she had to say. She felt the water as it reached her ankles and she began to scream as it moved up her legs. She tried to jump out of the chair, but the heavy blanket Roger had wrapped her in weighed her down as it soaked in the water. Even with all of her strength it would have been too much for her to fight for her life; weakened as she was, it was impossible.

She felt the water rise up to her chest, to her throat and then over her face. She coughed and sputtered as water began filling in her lungs. The blanket slipped off and she was finally free from the chair, but all she could do was panic and flail in the water as Roger turned around and started walking back toward the house. She screamed at him to help her before all of her strength was gone, and she sank helplessly to the bottom of the lake.

Not once, during all that time, did Roger turn to look back in her direction.

* * *

Roger and Emily met in the summer of 1897, when they were both 21. Roger had just graduated from the University of the South with a degree in English literature and Emily had just returned from a long trip overseas. Their parents were casual social acquaintances who decided that it was time for their children to get married.

To this end a dinner party was held at Roger's family home and Roger and Emily were instantly smitten when they met.

Emily was immediately attracted to his sharp features and his low-key but confident manner. She liked that he had studied English at school, which meant he was more interested in the development of his mind rather than his physical attributes or his financial interests. But what she loved most about him was how quiet he was when he ate his soup. Her father had been a noisy slurper all her life and she had long vowed not to marry any man who made irritating sounds while he ate.

As for Roger, he saw in Emily what all men saw in her: a slim, beautiful young woman with a startling and fascinating grace that made all who saw it want to protect it, no matter the cost. She also proved to be witty and agreeable, which made her more perfect in his eyes than he had ever previously considered humanly possible.

Much to their parents' delight, they were engaged within a week of their dinner party. They married a month later and started a new life as a couple. Both of their families were wealthy, so Roger had the luxury of choosing whatever profession most interested him. He decided he wanted to try his hand at writing, and he told his new bride that he wanted to find a tranquil place for them to live where a man of words could work properly.

Emily remembered the large mansion in Chattanooga where her grandparents used to live. It was situated beside a lake, across from the Greenwood Cemetery. Emily had always loved going there when she was a girl. Whenever she closed her eyes and thought of her perfect home, it was the one she saw in her mind. She worked hard to convince Roger that it was the perfect place for him to be a writer, and when he saw it, he knew she was right. Luckily, her parents had inherited the property after her grandparents had passed on, so it was merely a matter of moving in.

Their first five years there were the best of their entire lives. Roger wrote five novels, two of which were mildly successful, and Emily busied herself decorating and caring for their home and tending to her husband. He often threatened to hire a maid so she wouldn't have to work so hard, but she in turn made it clear that as long as she could stand, no one else would manage her household.

But as perfect as those years seemed, Emily and Roger had their occasional conflicts. Emily's favorite color was green and she employed it frequently throughout the house, a move that annoyed Roger, who disliked the color and felt it had a negative effect on his creativity. He insisted that their bedroom upstairs be decorated with a calming yellow wallpaper, even though Emily thought it was the ugliest thing she had ever seen. They occasionally fought over money, as Roger tended to spend it much faster than he earned it and Emily didn't like being so dependent on their parents' funds. But for the most part they were compatible and spent much of their time engaging in the kind of idle romantic activities enjoyed by the young.

It was during one of these idle larks in the nearby cemetery that Emily informed Roger that he was going to be a father. He found himself so overcome with joy when he heard the news that he had to jump onto the nearby footpath to avoid being so rude as to dance on someone's grave. While to many people, the Greenwood Cemetery would seem an odd place to share this wonderful news, Emily could think of no better spot. To her, the place was homage to one's ancestors, so it seemed the perfect place to celebrate the coming of a new life; it reinforced the beauty and tradition of the adventure on which they were now embarking. They were starting a family, which meant—even after their bodies were laid to rest in the ground in the cemetery where they now stood—they would live forever as a part of the lineage that would follow them in the future.

Their joy, though, was short lived. One morning, eight months into her pregnancy, Emily collapsed while she was working in the kitchen. Roger heard her fall and he ran to her and was horrified to see blood staining her legs. Terrified, he ran to the home of his nearest neighbor half a mile away. He urged them to find a doctor so he could return to Emily and make sure she was okay until they arrived.

When the doctor came, Roger could tell by the look on the man's face that the situation was grim; he not only risked losing his child but his beloved wife as well. It was the longest and most painful night of his life, and it ended with both great joy and tremendous sadness. Emily lived but their child died.

Emily had not been conscious during all of this, so it was up to Roger to tell her what had happened to their baby. She was inconsolable and wept for as long as she could remain awake. She stayed in her bed for two weeks and collapsed again when she finally tried to leave it. When the doctor came, she complained of a horrible pain in her legs and of a constant chill in her bones. He told them that she would have to stay in bed until her symptoms went away. And there she stayed for months and months, until a half a year had passed and it became clear that she might never leave her bed again.

Roger was ill equipped to deal with his wife's illness, but he could not bring himself to hire someone else to care for her. Though it had faded in the past few months, she still bore the grace that she had when they first met, and it still compelled him to do everything he could to protect her. But as the months passed, the pressure of his duties started taking their toll. There were moments—ones he instantly regretted—where he found himself resenting his wife and her constant fragility. But more than anything, he was lonely. At the best of times, Emily was listless and distracted and lacked any of the wit and sparkle that had once so attracted him. It got to the point where he was so starved for companionship that he found himself sneaking out of the house at night to go to the nearest saloon, a place he once thought of as the lowest kind of enterprise.

It was at this saloon, The Sweet Sally, where he met Rosie, a young barmaid from England who worked for tips and who wasn't above spending the night with any gentleman who had an extra dollar or two to hand her way. She wasn't a beautiful woman, but her cheeks were well served by her name and she had a warm laugh that sounded like music to Roger's ears since his life was now so consumed by so much grim silence. It didn't take long for Rosie to notice his affection for her and she worked hard to see it grow, in the hopes it might lead to bigger things in her future. One night, when he had drunk far

more than he ever had before, she convinced him to stay
the night in her tiny room above the saloon. There she
showed him a warmth and a tenderness that had been
missing from his life ever since that horrible day when
Emily collapsed. He left in the middle of the night, afraid
to not be home when his wife awoke that morning, but he
returned the next day and offered Rosie a job as his
housekeeper. The weekly wage he suggested was more
than double what she earned in a month at the saloon,
so she agreed without hesitation. His only request was
that she stay very quiet while she worked and never go
upstairs, which she was more than happy to agree to, since
it meant cutting her workload by half.

Despite what he would eventually tell Emily, Rosie did
not come to the house three times a week. She moved in
and stayed permanently in the old servants' wing downstairs, where Roger would frequently join her. One night
when he was curled up beside her, Rosie began to whisper
ideas into his head.

"That poor thing. My heart goes out to her," Rosie said.

"Who is that?" he asked, barely awake.

"Your wife, silly. I can't imagine what it's like to be
stuck in that bed like that. I can't even think about it too
long or else I'll start to get the chills. I just wish there was
something we could do for her."

"Me too," he mumbled.

"If I were in her state, I would pray night and day that
someone would come and put me out of my misery. It
would be the kindest thing, but there are few men out
there brave enough to take that risk."

"What risk?"

"Putting me out of my misery, like I said. Some would call it murder, but I don't. It isn't murder if it's the right thing to do, but I suppose the law sees it differently."

The word "murder" struck a chord in Roger and caused him to sit up in the bed.

"What are you saying?" he asked his mistress, not quite willing to believe what she was implying.

"I'm not saying anything," she protested. "I just think that a good man would not allow his wife to suffer so long in a room all by herself. It isn't proper. Especially if it becomes clear that she's never going to recover."

"Rose, I could never kill my wife."

"It's not killing if it's the proper thing to do," she insisted. "There isn't a person alive who would let a dog suffer like that woman suffers, but you're more than happy to keep her up there, trapped in her own endless misery."

Roger's voice grew dark. "Rose, be quiet. You should not say such things."

"I should if they need to be said! Are you a man, Roger Devore? Are you a man?"

"Rosie, be quiet! Emily might hear you!"

"I won't be quiet! Not while that poor woman suffers. It is monstrous what you do! Monstrous! You keep her here, when it is clear that she no longer wishes to live, because you are too weak to do the right thing. I have never in my life seen such cowardice! It sickens me. It sickens me because in my heart I know you are a good man and no good man would let her horror continue!"

Roger was so angry that he could not speak; instead he drew his hand back and slapped Rosie as hard as he could. She burst into tears and ran out of the room, while he sat there on the bed and felt a horrible sickness in the bottom of his stomach.

Rosie waited for three weeks before she risked broaching the subject of Roger's ailing wife once again. They were sitting in the dining room, eating supper, when—after a long silence—she decided it was time to make another move.

"It's only right that she should know," she said out of nowhere.

"What are you talking about?" asked Roger.

"About us—about me. A woman suffers like that, she should at least know her husband has found another."

"You wouldn't—" he said.

"It would be a relief for her, I'm sure. She must be worried sick about what she's doing to you and she'd be happy to know you've found someone to take over all of her wifely duties."

"I swear to God—"

"I can only imagine what she must have done to earn such scorn and hatred from her own husband, who would rather see her slowly wither and rot than know a moment of true happiness."

"Stop it!" he shouted.

From up above them they heard the barest whisper of a sound. It was Emily.

Roger jumped out of his chair and ran upstairs to see her.

"Roger, what's going on?" she asked him weakly. "I just heard you shouting."

"It was nothing, Emily," he insisted. "A stray cat has found a way into the house and he keeps jumping onto my desk as I'm writing. I shouted at him to scare him away."

"Really? What kind of cat was it?"

"I didn't notice. A gray one, I think."

"Gray isn't a breed," she told him.

"Well, I don't know much about cats, but I do know I shouldn't have raised my voice like that. Not while you're napping."

"I wasn't really napping," she said. "I've been too busy thinking about something."

"And what is that, my dear?"

"You. I'm worried about you being alone all of the time. It isn't healthy."

"I'm fine," he said, slightly taken aback by the timing of this confession.

"You should go out. Make some friends. It doesn't do you any good to spend your time playing nursemaid to me."

"Has somebody been in here to talk to you?"

"No. What a strange question. Why do you ask?"

He shook his head. "No reason. You just didn't sound like yourself for a moment."

"Who did I sound like?"

"I don't know. Someone else."

She smiled and raised her hand to his cheek and looked into his eyes. "Roger, are you crying?"

He got up and wiped his tears from his face. "No, I think I'm allergic to that damn cat."

"Yes, that makes sense," she said. She looked up and saw the wall in front of her and sighed. "I don't know what you were thinking when you chose that wallpaper. It really is the ugliest thing I've ever seen. Sometimes I don't think I could bear to look at it for another minute longer."

Roger turned and faced the doorway and looked into the hall. "Do you ever have days when you think you'll never get out of this bed?" he asked.

"Yes," she answered.

"How does that make you feel?" He braced himself for whatever she said next.

"On those days, on those very darkest of days, I admit that I wonder if maybe it wouldn't have been better if I had died that night. Does that sound horrible?" she asked.

"No, it doesn't."

That night Rosie explained to him how it should be done. "They'll have no choice but to think it was an accident," she said confidently when she was done.

"I don't know if I can go through with it," said Roger.

"It's for the best," she insisted. "When the time comes, you'll know that and it will be easy."

"Easy?"

She nodded. "Easy."

* * *

Rosie had been wrong. It had not been easy at all. It had been the hardest thing Roger had ever done, but beyond this one mistake, everything else she had predicted proved correct. The authorities ruled the drowning an accident and they even hailed Roger a hero for attempting to save her when he supposedly came back from the house. If they suspected the truth, they never gave their suspicions away with a look, word or gesture.

Roger managed to fool them, even though he was disgusted by what he had done. After the funeral, Emily was buried in the plot she had always wanted in the Greenwood Cemetery. He threatened to kick Rosie out of the house because looking at her was a constant reminder of his horrible crime, but she told him she would go directly to the police if he didn't marry her when it was socially proper to do so. He had no choice but to give in, and they were married six months later. Her first two acts as his bride were to hire a maid so she would never have to clean anything ever again, and to completely redecorate the entire house. The only room she left untouched was the bedroom where Emily had spent the last year of her life.

"I love this wallpaper. It's the only decent thing she put up in the entire house," she said to Roger.

Roger refused to sleep in the room, preferring to stay in the room he had slept in ever since Emily had first taken ill. Rosie didn't mind, as she had already gotten everything that she wanted from him at that point. During the nights that followed, he started having horrible nightmares that left him in terrible agony whenever he awoke. His legs would ache and he would shiver from the chill that would not leave his bones. These dreams soon became so bad that he took to trying to stay awake at night, doing whatever he could to fight off his need to sleep.

One night, he threw on his night coat and wandered outside down to the lake. He had avoided the spot ever since the night he killed his beloved wife, but now for some reason he felt himself drawn inexorably to it. Though it was warm out, he could not get rid of the chill that surrounded him. He looked out over the water and noticed that there was a strange green mist hovering over the lake. He had never seen anything like it before. The scent of it started to make him feel queasy, so he kneeled down to stop from passing out. There he saw in the ground

206 Ghost Stories of Tennessee

two long tracks in the earth, identical to those that he had left behind that night he took Emily out to the lake in her wheelchair. Then he swore he could hear the sound of someone splashing and struggling in the water in front of him. He looked up and saw that the lake was empty.

Your mind is starting to play tricks on you, he thought.

He turned to walk away when he heard the sound of a woman screaming and begging for help. This time he could not stop himself from looking back. No one was there. He froze when he saw a green haze floating in front of him. Its shape was human and its voice instantly recognizable.

"Roger, you'll be joining me shortly," it said.

Roger screamed and ran through the haze toward his home. He threw the door open and ran into his living room, where he found Rosie standing with a large, fierce-looking man.

His words hampered by his lack of breath. "What's going on?" he asked.

"Is this him?" asked the man.

"That's him." Rosie nodded and pointed at Roger. "He's the one who's been beating me."

"What are you talking about?" asked Roger.

The man punched him in the face, knocking him off of his feet. "Scum like you shouldn't be allowed to talk to a fine woman such as this!"

Dazed, Roger remained on the ground as the much larger man towered over him.

"I don't know what you're talking about," he said.

"A man who hits a woman isn't a man at all," the man said sternly.

"But I've never touched her!"

"See how he lies!" Rosie ran to the man and grabbed his shoulder. "It started before we were even married, when he kept me here as his mistress with his wife upstairs. I spoke in her defense and he slapped me harder than anyone ever has before, and it's only gotten worse since then."

"She's lying!" Roger cried. "It's true I did hit her once, when she told me to kill my wife, but I've never touched her since!"

"You are as loathsome a maggot as I've ever seen!" cursed the man as he bent over to pick Roger up.

Roger eluded the man's grasp, leapt to his feet and ran out of the house. Before he could even think about it, he found himself once again on the edge of the lake. There he saw the small rowboat he and Emily used to paddle in to get to the cemetery on the other side. He jumped into the boat and started rowing as fast as he could. By the time the man chasing him got to the lake, Roger was already halfway to the other side.

He was so busy rowing that he failed to notice the green mist that started gathering around the lake. At first it stretched out over the entire surface of the water and then it quickly inched forward toward Roger's boat. Soon it formed into the haze that Roger had seen earlier; it lifted itself off the water and floated into the boat.

"Roger," it said.

Roger looked up with a start and stopped rowing. "What are you?" he cried.

"What do you think I am?" it cried back. "You threw me so cruelly into these waters! I am the spirit of the one you abandoned for the warmth of another's bed! I am the heart you crushed because you lacked the will it took to wait—"

"Stop!" he shouted. "What are you going to do to me?"

"I told you, Roger. I said you were going to be joining me soon, but even I had no idea that it would be *this* soon."

The haze started moving quickly back and forth, causing the boat to rock unsteadily. The momentum grew until the boat finally turned over and Roger splashed into the cold water. He tried to swim to the surface, but something held him under. No matter how much he fought against it, he could not rise, and within a minute all of his fight was gone. He succumbed to the blissful peace that is said to come over those who drown.

It was Rosie who called the authorities, telling them that her husband decided to cross the lake to visit the grave of his first wife when the boat toppled over. They saw no reason to investigate further and the case was closed. Rosie was horrified to discover that her late husband's wealth was not really his own. It turned out that Emily's parents still owned the mansion they were living in, and the money Roger made as a writer was almost all gone, with very little else was expected to come in, as the two successful novels he had written were now out of fashion and set to go out of print. Within six months she was back at The Sweet Sally, no better off than she was before she met Roger.

Roger was buried beside Emily in the Greenwood Cemetery, joining her just as the voice of the green haze had predicted. Emily's parents sold the house not long after, and its new owners claimed that some nights they could see a green mist over the water, but other nights the mist was yellow.

The End